A Stoic Guidebook for Recovery

Ancient Philosophy for a Better Life After Addiction

DEREK CASTLEMAN
&
EPICTETUS

Title: A Stoic Guidebook for Recovery: Ancient Philosophy for a Better Life After Addiction

Author: Derek Castleman
ISBN: **Paperback Edition**: 9798856267524
      Hardcover Edition: 9798856267999

Cover Design: Muhammad Kaleem
Editor: Fatima Alishba
Publisher: Sober Stoic Books
Printed in United States
First Printing: 2023
For permissions or further inquiries, please contact:
derekcastleman@gmail.com

Disclaimer: The information provided in this book is for general informational purposes only and is not intended as a substitute for professional medical advice, diagnosis, or treatment. Always seek the advice of your physician or other qualified health care provider with any questions you may have regarding a medical condition or treatment and before undertaking a new health care regimen. The author and publisher are not responsible for any adverse effects or consequences resulting from the use of any suggestions or procedures described in this book.

This book is dedicated to Brian, Jared, Cecil, Scott, Nate, Steve and the brothers of Chandler Lodge who are still with us and the others that I will meet once again in the great beyond.

Table of Contents

Introduction – A Stoic Recovery 1

Part One – Philosophy, Stoicism, and the Tales of Two Writers 7
Philosophy of Life.. 9
The Backbone of Stoicism 17
Epictetus.. 22
My Story... 25

Part Two – The Enchiridion: Expanded for a Stoic Recovery 35
Some Quick Notes on Part Two 37
Chapter 1 – The Serenity Prayer 39
Chapter 2 – The Dangers of Desire and Aversion 49
Chapter 3 – Preparing for Loss.. 56
Chapter 4 – Expect the Expected... 62
Chapter 5 – Judge Events Correctly... 67
Chapter 6 – The Slippery Slope of Pride 74
Chapter 7 – Be Prepared for Death's Voyage 79
Chapter 8 – Wish for All That Happens 83
Chapter 9 – There Is No Excuse 87
Chapter 10 – Strength Through Adversity 91
Chapter 11 – We Borrow That Which We Possess 95
Chapter 12 – Practicing Indifference for Peace of Mind 99
Chapter 13 – Courage to Be Different 106
Chapter 14 – Only Blame Yourself 110
Chapter 15 – The Feast of Life 116
Chapter 16 – The Grief of Others... 122
Chapter 17 – The Universal Play.. 125
Chapter 18 – There Is No Such Thing as Bad Luck............................ 129
Chapter 19 – Become Unconquerable... 132
Chapter 20 – Anger Is a Choice.. 139
Chapter 21 – Premeditation of Trouble 146

Chapter 22 – Stay Focused Despite the Naysayers 151

Chapter 23 – Be Content With Yourself 156

Chapter 24 – You Are Somebody 159

Chapter 25 – No Reason to Be Jealous 168

Chapter 26 – Listen to Your Own Advice 173

Chapter 27 – Evil Is Within 176

Chapter 28 – Own Your Mind 180

Chapter 29 – Know What It Will Take 183

Chapter 30 – Do Your Duty 192

Chapter 31 – Stop Blaming God (Nature) 196

Chapter 32 – Seeing Into the Future 202

Chapter 33 – Ways in Which to Live Like a Stoic 207

Chapter 34 – Dealing With Temptation 222

Chapter 35 – Courage in What You Do 226

Chapter 36 – Consideration of Others 229

Chapter 37 – Do What You Do Best 232

Chapter 38 – Protect Your Mind 237

Chapter 39 – Never Enough 240

Chapter 40 – Stoicism Is for Everyone 245

Chapter 41 – Workout Your Mind 248

Chapter 42 – When Someone Thinks Wrong of You 252

Chapter 43 – Grab Onto the Right Handle 255

Chapter 44 – Don't Judge a Book by Its Cover 258

Chapter 45 – Stop Assuming the Why 262

Chapter 46 – Actions Speak Louder Than Words 266

Chapter 47 – Only You Need to Know 271

Chapter 48 – How You Can Tell You Are Living It 274

Chapter 49 – Knowing Is Not Enough 281

Chapter 50 – Don't Break Your Laws 285

Chapter 51 – The Time Is Now 288

Chapter 52 – Focus on Doing First and Foremost 293

Chapter 53 – What Guides Epictetus 297

Literature Cited 299

A Stoic Recovery

My name is Derek.

And I am an alcoholic.

And drugs are part of my story as well.

And sex.

And codependency.

And being bipolar.

The list can go on...and on...and on.

However, I am also a philosopher...a Stoic philosopher, to be more exact.

A little over a year into my recovery, I felt stagnant. I was long past that pink cloud phase of recovery and coming down to earth hard and fast. My old ways of thinking were creeping back into my life. I was most likely heading in the infamous "dry drunk" direction. Or even worse...relapse (again).

It was frustrating.

It would be nearly at the same time that my girlfriend and one of my housemates at my sober living would recommend me to read this philosophy known as Stoicism. I do not know if it was fate... chance...or merely they both saw the same thing happening to me. But somehow, and for some reason, two people I cared deeply about in life and respected their opinions suggested me to investigate this philosophy.

So, I did what most people do.

I Googled it.

And it instantly fascinated me.

I would discover that everything I was reading about how this philosophy described life and a better way to live made complete sense to me. It gave me a new way to view the world and how to use this new understanding to live a better life no matter what situation I found myself in. This was particularly useful to me at the time since I had been jobless, living in a small room at a sober living, and had a girlfriend I had been with for years and wanted to marry but did not have enough money to be able to do so.

So then, as a sign of the addict that still reigns inside me, I immediately began buying numerous Stoicism books, diving into whatever I could grasp of the knowledge it had to convey and then applying it to my life.

Stoicism is a philosophy of life that dates back to Ancient Greece, around 300 B.C. It would eventually find its way to Ancient Rome, where many of its well-known philosophers would expand on the meaning and practice. At its core, Stoicism focused on living a virtuous life, seeking excellence in character in all you do. To do this, a person needs to:

- Learn what is truly valuable in life.
- Handle and control negative emotions (because these can affect our ability to make good decisions).
- Properly handle desires and passions that can carry us away.
- Understand what we have control over and what we don't.

Principles and practices that I found I needed to learn in recovery.

Cures for the causes of my disease of addiction.

Now, some might think, what could these people who lived nearly two thousand years ago know what it is like to live today?

The answer is, surprisingly, 'a lot.'

There is this saying, "The more things change, the more they stay the same." And when I read the works of the Ancient Stoics, I could not help how often this saying kept coming up in my mind. Even though the world has dramatically changed technologically and through human advancement since their time, human nature and behavior have changed little.

People behaved the same way back then as they do now. You will read about people struggling with anger, grief, anxiety, and depression. You will discover how worrying about the future and what it may hold and dwelling on past mistakes has long been a part of the human experience.

Struggles with addiction.

Worries about reputation.

Greed and lust for power.

I even laughed at the Stoic philosopher Seneca describing people's love for their chariots, similar to how people treat their cars today.

It is these commonalities in human nature that allow this philosophy to be just as helpful today as it was when it was first explored and written. The fact that we still find the works of the Ancient Stoics in publications today suggests that people throughout history must have found some value in their insights into life. Even the work *Meditations* by Marcus Aurelius was simply a personal journal he had kept, yet you can find it on bookshelves worldwide.

Historically, you can find examples where people were saying things very similar to the philosophy because they had either read it themselves or had found similar conclusions about life in their own way. An example of this could be The Serenity Prayer, which was uniquely said and lived by the Stoics long before being written.

The leading pioneers of Cognitive Behavior Therapy (CBT) admitted the central role of Stoicism in their development of it (Donaldson 2020, 16). People who have seen therapists or experienced rehab for their addictions may have had some exposure to CBT. This form of therapy is one of the primary treatments for addiction, suggesting that the philosophy would have useful applications for individuals seeking recovery.

For people who practice a 12 Step form of recovery, you can easily find each of the steps interwoven within the philosophy. Or maybe you are following a Buddhist program; in that case, you will discover the Eightfold Path embedded within it. And one of the key advantages of Stoicism is that it is a philosophy and not a religion, so it can be followed by individuals of any religious faith or even those who choose not to have one.

In recent decades, a resurgence in studying and practicing Stoic philosophy has culminated in a movement known as Modern Stoicism. New books are being published each year. Podcasts are being created. And you can find thousands of people online discussing how they are using this philosophy to navigate life in this modern world.

Shortly after getting into Stoicism, I began scouring the internet for other people who had used this philosophy to help them recover. And I found some. But not many. There were various articles here and there where people had also discovered how Stoicism could help them in recovery, but there was no primary go-to source.

I began conversing with some modern Stoic writers, asking them questions to better understand using it for recovery. They would advise and help me out in their responses as best as they could. However, at the same time, they would have to admit they do not know what it is like to go through addiction and recovery.

I would eventually begin social media accounts under the name The Sober Stoic, where I shared different quotes with people in recovery and found others interested in it. I even created a blog where I discussed how I used the philosophy to help my recovery. In addition, I would talk to people at meetings with similar struggles in their sobriety, and I found that insights from the philosophy could help them as well.

So why this book?

I wanted to create a primary source for people who have struggled with addiction and are traversing the path of recovery. I wanted to give them a chance that I did not have in my Stoic recovery; a source where they can learn about this philosophy and how to harness it to strengthen their journey.

The first part of this book will introduce you to philosophy in general, with most of the attention placed on the purpose of a philosophy of life, a philosophical category that Stoicism is placed under. Then, I will briefly introduce the basics of Stoicism and the Four Cardinal Virtues embedded within it. Finally, I will conclude with the life stories of the two writers of this book, myself and Epictetus.

The second part, and the primary purpose of this book, will center on the *Enchiridion*. This manual or handbook is based on the teachings of the Ancient Roman Stoic philosopher Epictetus and has been a must-read for anyone wanting to learn the philosophy for over two thousand years. It is divided into fifty-three chapters, ranging from a single sentence to several paragraphs. It provides a guide to Stoic principles and practices and the logic behind them.

For each chapter, I will add information that expands on how it relates to the deeper parts of Stoic philosophy, addiction, and recovery. I will draw on my life experiences, the commonalities we can find in our shared stories, and what we learn in recovery programs. In addition, I will present quotes from other Stoic writers (Ancient Roman and modern) and provide information from addiction specialists, psychiatrists, and research studies.

By the end, you will have read one of the most well-known Ancient Stoic books and hopefully can see how it could relate to your own experiences with addiction and recovery.

Whether or not you follow a specific recovery program, I hope you discover that what you read in this book can relate to your chosen path and can become another source to strengthen your journey.

Welcome to A Stoic Guidebook for Recovery.

I hope this will help your journey toward a better life.

PART ONE

Philosophy, Stoicism, and the Tales of Two Writers

Philosophy of Life

"What do you want out of life...of the things in life you might pursue, which is the thing you believe to be the most valuable?"
– William B. Irvine, A Guide to the Good Life, pg. 1.

What do you want out of life? Have you ever honestly asked yourself that question and answered it thoroughly? If you saw that question and thought of answers like:

- The job you want to do.
- The house you want to live in.
- A car you want.
- Maybe a spouse or children.

Well, these are the things you want in your life, the goals you have laid out for yourself. It is easy for people to list off what they want in life but not so much what they want out of life. It is easy to spring quickly to answers like these since we have been trained to be this way. In school and sometimes by parents, we get asked what we want to be someday (I even catch myself doing this with my daughter). The correct answer is that future dream job we envision for ourselves. Life surrounds us with advertisements that show us what to own or do to be happier. And now, because of social media, we have FOMO (fear of missing out); we see the lives of others and think we are missing out as we compare ourselves to them.

The world thrives on what we want in life.

But is that enough?

And what happens when you have finished your checklist?

At one point in my life, I had the wife, the child, the house, the career, the car, and many of the things I wanted to own. But it always seemed like something was missing--this emptiness of not feeling complete. There had to be more to this because getting what I wanted in life was not enough.

Drugs and alcohol became an excellent way to fill that void in my life. And I know I am not alone in this feeling; countless others in recovery have experienced similar sentiments. Some who once battled addiction described having achieved seemingly everything they desired in life, only to find it still left them yearning for more.

And this is not just an issue for addicts.

Unhappiness is a widespread phenomenon. A recent poll found that only 14% of Americans felt "very happy" in 2020, down from 31% in 2018 (Associated Press 2020). And even though that low number in 2020 could be attributed to the pandemic, it still shows that far less than half of the population felt "very happy" before it.

It is why we have this rise and dominance of the self-improvement industry. You can learn how to build self-esteem, lose weight, get rich, find love, and become successful if you spend the money. Something missing in life? This industry will make it better for you. It is a ten-billion-dollar industry offering quick fixes to what you feel you are missing in life, with one caveat. They don't want you to fully improve since they will lose a customer (Jones n.d.).

It is almost similar in style to some of us in recovery, who are now sober and want our lives to improve and return to how they used to be as quickly as possible. There is a reason we are told "easy does it" in recovery; these things take time. And the most important things take a lifetime.

Now let's return to that original question.

What do you want out of life?

The answer to this question will be the basis of your philosophy of life. It is what you see the meaning of life to be as well as the way you should live it. There are several parts to your philosophy of life. First, it will include a metaphysical role in how you view the world and universe you live in, the laws that guide it, and your part within it. Then, there is the ethical part, the code by which you have decided to live your life using the knowledge you gained from the first part. This ethics will include things such as:

- What you find to be valuable.
- How you will deal with the challenges that come your way.
- How you respond to moral dilemmas.

The ethical part is the guide for how you move throughout your days. Finally, of course, there must be a plan of action for how you will live by this code.

Your philosophy of life is your purpose, and how do you live it?

It is a goal we can never complete because it is one we should practice daily until our last moments. Yet, it is that goal we can check in on every day to see if we are living the life we want. And the reason we must know our philosophy of life is that "there is a danger that you will mislive - that despite all your activity, despite all the pleasant diversions you might have enjoyed while alive, you will end up living a bad life" (Irving 2009, 1-2). Because without this target to aim towards, we run the danger of squandering the time that we have on this planet, wandering aimlessly without that lifelong guiding purpose for all that we do.

It was crucial that I discover a philosophy of life in my recovery. During my addictions, I never saw a purpose in my daily life. I bounced around from pleasant diversion to pleasant diversion, never understanding the meaning behind each day I lived. The goals I had laid out for myself in my younger years had been pretty much accomplished, leaving me to wonder what I should aim for next. I had no reason for the actions that I was committing. And as my life spiraled downward, being metaphysically empty meant my life felt meaningless.

Without a code to live by and a plan of action, I did things that I was perfectly fine doing in my addiction, but I can't imagine how I could do such things in my sobriety. I felt so useless to the world and degenerate that I suffered from suicidal thoughts. Living daily without a philosophy of life became the guide to the dark depths of my addiction. Therefore, it became essential to find one in my recovery to ensure I do not get led back there.

"In fifteen and a half years of schooling, I learned math, physics, chemistry, biology, and a bunch of other stuff, except how to deal with challenging situations? How to face my fears and struggles? What to do about my depressive feelings? How to deal effectively with the death of my friend? What to do with my anger? How to be more confident? Nope, I must have missed all those classes."
– Jonas Salzgeber, The Little Book of Stoicism, pg. 2.

All the years of schooling and the massive quantities of knowledge shoved into developing minds will only prove valuable depending on life choices made further down the road in adulthood.

As a chemistry teacher, I had to debate with students when they would ask me how they would use this information in their lives. And honestly, many of the students I taught had other aspirations that would not require the use of chemistry to the extent that I taught it to them. Some basics, like knowing what an acid or base is and chemical safety, can be helpful but ask yourselves how often you use Stoichiometry and Avogadro's number.

However, what about the subjects in which we learn to live? Where do we learn how to:

- Face challenges.
- Deal with negative emotions.
- Build self-esteem.
- Make the right decisions.
- Discuss the purpose of life or even how to accept the death that we face or that of our loved ones.

These are the things that everyone needs to learn because, inevitably, we will all experience them.

Philosophy is the subject in which to learn those things.

And there was a time in which it was widely learned.

During the days of Ancient Greece and Rome, schools of philosophy were found throughout cities where parents could send their children to get an education on how to live. In those days, philosophy was not a subject you just learned but would become your way of life. And to be a philosopher was not because you taught the subject but because you lived it.

It was a subject of action.

The school of philosophy you would attend would become the philosophy of life you would follow. It would help you discover what you want out of life, the ethical code you might live by, and how you might answer the questions posed by Jonas Salzgeber above.

And it was not like there was just one option for school to attend. There were multiple ones to select from, each having its way of metaphysically and ethically describing the world in which we live. You could find the one that worked the best for you. A few notable schools were:

- The Cyrenaics, who might sound familiar to addicts, focused on the purpose of life being about moment-to-moment bodily pleasure, although they did advocate for self-control.
- The Epicureans also focused on life being about pleasure. Although, they looked at it not just being moment-to-moment but on a long-term basis while noting the importance of mental satisfaction compared to physical pleasure.
- The Cynics viewed that the purpose of life was a virtuous one that was in accordance with nature, which often meant living a very frugal lifestyle and rejecting various social norms (look up Diogenes of Sinope if you want to learn about a fascinating character in history).
- The Stoics also believed in living a virtuous life, but unlike the Cynics, they saw it as one in which you practice being a part of society and do not have to reject all external goods.

These are just a few of the schools that existed. You should be able to see how each attempted to define the overall purpose for life, and the one you chose would then shape how you would approach life situations daily.

When I speak about philosophy to some people, they discuss with me their philosophy is the religion they follow. And this line of thinking can make sense. During the Middle Ages, Christianity absorbed parts of the way of living aspects of philosophy (Hadot 1995, 107). The overtaking of philosophy by religion would push the subject towards the realm of conceptual, making it the more academic subject we are familiar with today. However, William Irvine brings up a few interesting points in his book *A Guide to the Good Life*. First, he discusses how religion tells a person how to be good, what to do and not to do, and how to get into the afterlife (Irvine 2009, 22-23). However, concepts of living a good life and what a person should pursue or not pursue are left to the followers to figure out. So, it would be perfectly fine for one person to live in a mansion and drive an expensive car and another person of the same faith to live in a hut and ride a bicycle. If both followed the religion's rules, they would end up in the same place in the afterlife.

He furthers his point by discussing that if religion discussed these concepts of what was worth pursuing and not pursuing in life, we should see differences between people of different faiths. Yet, we see people from various religions having parallel lives in what they seek. The houses, the careers, and the things they want to buy. You cannot tell the difference in religion simply by their lifestyle.

Roughly 75% of Americans describe themselves as having a religion they follow (Pew Center n.d.). Yet earlier, I discussed how only 14% of people report being "very happy" in life. Why such a wide discrepancy in numbers?

Could something be missing?

Religion and philosophy do not need to battle against each other. Both can work together. And the philosophy of life that you choose to live by can help to supplement and practice your faith more deeply and profoundly. At different times, you can read Stoics discussing a belief in God; at other times, they simply discuss the nature of the universe itself. The *Enchiridion*, the focus of this book, had three Christian adaptations for use in monastic life. And from my readings into Buddhism, I found aspects of Stoicism in each part of the Noble Eightfold Path. As you read this book, I hope you can see how it does not negate whatever you believe in, religious or non-religious, but helps strengthen it in your pursuit of a better life.

Whether you choose Stoicism as your philosophy of life after reading this book, the most important thing I want you to take away from this chapter is that you should take a moment to think about the one you want to live. Then, be able to answer the questions of:

1. What do you want out of life?
2. What is your purpose in this world?
3. What code do you live by to guide your daily actions?

The worst thing that could happen is that you never think of such things as these and come to the end of your life realizing you never understood how to live. And I do not know about you, but I lost too much time to my addictions to throw any more of it away in my recovery.

The Backbone of Stoicism

W hat do you want out of life?

A Stoic would say to live a virtuous one.

Excellence of character.

It does not matter what job you have...what you own, or how much money you have in the bank...married or single...children or none...well respected or not. The purpose is to come to the end of your life, look back on it, and realize that you lived a good life because you lived to be the best person you could be.

No regrets.

You lived to be a better person each day. The things that matter in life are what you valued. You made the right decisions at the right time. You treated all humans with fairness and without judgments. When you chose your goals, you tried your hardest to achieve them, even if you could not. And you realized that the time you were given to be alive was precious, and you stopped wasting it.

The beauty of living a life focused on excellence of character is that you will get some fantastic side effects through the process, which are very beneficial to those who have gone through addiction:

- You will learn to stop harming other people and doing the wrong things in life.

- The part of Step 10 in which you promptly admit you have done something wrong will be less of an occurrence (you will still mess up since we are human, but it should become less frequent).
- You will gain greater self-esteem as you realize your inner value and what you bring to the world.

I enjoy the constant feeling of tranquility I live with each day. Whatever struggles I may face that life throws at me no longer has negative effects as I have a constant sense of calm, knowing that I am living the best me I could be.

One of the most empowering aspects of basing your life's purpose on the excellence of character is its accessibility to everyone. It does not matter if you are rich or poor, healthy or sick, free or imprisoned, have a home, or are homeless. It is something that you can fulfill no matter what situation in life you find yourself in.

Your purpose for living will always be there.

Epictetus knew this personally since he had lived a part of his life as an enslaved person. Musonius Rufus discovered this when he was exiled from his homeland to the harsh environment on an island in the Mediterranean Sea. And James Bond Stockdale learned this when he used the teachings of Epictetus to survive being a prisoner of war during the Vietnam War.

The overall purpose of Stoicism is to live a virtuous life, but the Stoics would break this up into four parts to help lead to this goal. These would be called the Four Cardinal Virtues or the Four Pillars of Stoicism. These four virtues are **wisdom**, **justice**, **courage**, and **temperance**. Looking at these four, you could possibly begin to make connections to how they relate to recovery programs you may have taken part in.

Wisdom focuses on understanding what is good and not good (bad); the judgments that we can make in life. Now you might think you already know the difference between these two. However, the Stoics have a different perspective, seeing bad only as something that comes from within the individual and not from others. A major part of the philosophy focuses on oneself rather than on what others are doing or saying. They also have a third category of indifferent—the things of no concern. So, Stoic wisdom comes down to knowing what is good, what is bad, and what is indifferent, then making the right decisions based on this understanding.

Justice is the duty we have towards others. Humans are social creatures. All the advances we have made throughout human history have mainly come from our ability to work together. And these days, humans are more interconnected than ever with globalization, worldwide ease of travel, satellite-linked communication, and massive cargo ships moving products across oceans. You most likely own things produced in other countries, which means you have affected the lives of people in those places. Understanding that humanity relies on each other, justice to Stoics is about doing what is right for other people, your community, and the world. You should be kind, respectful, understanding, fair, and generous in your interactions with others. And you should be this way no matter how they are acting. And when it comes to your community and the world, are you committing to actions to improve it? Stoic justice must be done in all you do, even during life's difficulties.

Justice requires courage. Can you do the right thing no matter what anyone says or does to deter you? Do you have the ability to do the right thing even though you might feel fear, anxiety, or the desire to do something else? Stoicism is a way of living different from the world surrounding you. Remember, others may have a different philosophy of living than you or none at all. So, it will take courage to commit to it and see it through in everything you do.

The last virtue, and probably the most beneficial to addicts, is temperance (moderation). It is the practice of self-restraint, self-control, and self-discipline. Live a life that is not one of excess with control over your impulses.

We should know that.

Our addictions were a life of impulsivity and excess. We know where that led us. And we need to ensure that we do not transfer those addictions to other areas of our lives in recovery.

A life of temperance is one in which you try to maintain control over your emotions. We should know the importance of this as well. A lack of control over emotions, especially negative ones, often fuels addictive behaviors.

The Four Cardinal virtues exist for each other.

They intertwine and rely on each other.

You can have the wisdom to know what is right or wrong. But justice will shape what you should do. However, it might take courage to carry through with what you decide. And without temperance, you might be so overcome with desires or emotions that you may not be able to determine the right thing to do and find yourself on the path of the wrong choice.

My philosophy of life is to be a virtuous person.

Okay.

But how?

It is easy to say that you want to be a good person and have a noble character, but what is the path to achieving that? The Four Cardinal Virtues are a way to break it down into simpler terms. They give you targets you can aim for to achieve the goal of being a virtuous person.

20

First, practice wisdom in your life. Second, commit to actions dedicated to the idea of justice. Third, have courage in the things that you do. Fourth, practice moderation and not be carried in the wrong direction. If you work on these four areas of your life, you will become the virtuous person you want.

Okay.

A lot easier said than done.

The purpose of this chapter was to give you an overview of Stoicism. Throughout the *Enchiridion*, which makes up the second part of this book, Epictetus will discuss how to incorporate each of the Four Cardinal Virtues in your life and give knowledge on why. And as he does this, remember, it is all focused on the overarching goal of living a virtuous life.

Epictetus

Being one writer of this book, I felt it only fitting that you would know about his life. When he speaks of being able to practice the philosophy no matter what hardships you may find yourself in, it comes from a man who had to endure difficulties many of us could never imagine experiencing.

Epictetus (50 CE – 135 CE) was born into slavery in Hierapolis, a Greek city. His original name is not even known, while the name they gave him was *epíkttos,* which means "acquired." He was known to have had a physical disability with his leg. However, it is not known why; it is commonly thought this was due to abuse from an enslaver.

He was brought to Rome when he was still young as an enslaved person by his master, who worked in the emperor's court. Epictetus was permitted to study philosophy by attending lectures by Musonius Rufus (a well-known Stoic at the time). And after the emperor's death, Epictetus would finally be granted his freedom. With the knowledge he had gained in his younger years, Epictetus would hold his own lectures in Rome. However, the Stoics angered the new emperor through their popularity and opposition to his tyranny. Leading many of them, Epictetus included, to be expelled from the city.

He would return to Greece, where he would live the rest of his life. He would set up his own school of philosophy and become widely known. People would travel long distances (even from Rome) to come and hear him speak. However, he continued to live a life of simplicity with very few possessions. He would never marry or have children of his own. But in his older years, he adopted a child who would have possibly died without his help.

It is not known how Epictetus died.

Epictetus wrote nothing himself. He just gave lectures. One of his students, Arrian, is responsible for any writings that bear his name. Arrian would become a well-known historian and write many works of his own. From Epictetus's teachings, he would create two works, *Discourses* and *Enchiridion* (the subject of this book). *Discourses* are more extended versions of Epictetus's lectures, while *Enchiridion* is a shorter handbook. When these works are compared to the other writings of Arrian, there are distinct differences in style and content, which gives support to these being the words of Epictetus himself.

Epictetus would significantly influence another Stoic named Marcus Aurelius. What is fascinating about this is that Marcus Aurelius was a Roman emperor (known as the last good Roman emperor). The journal that Marcus Aurelius wrote near the end of his life has been passed down through the years and can now be found published under *Meditations*. You can find him referring to the teachings of Epictetus in this work.

But think of what this means.

The most powerful and wealthiest man in Rome read the works of and was heavily influenced by a man born into slavery who lived a simple life.

This is the story of Epictetus. I wanted you to learn about his life before you read his teachings. Then, throughout the book's second part, you will get to know him better as you gain insight into his mind and what he believed.

My Story

In this final chapter of part one, I wanted to give you an understanding of my story. I guess you could call this my: *what it was like, what happened, what it is like now.*

I do this since you will often read me referring to my life throughout the rest of the book and how Stoicism helped. But I also want you to find yourself somewhat in my story. My favorite meetings are always speaker meetings, and I love reading the stories of others who have recovered from addiction. It makes me not feel so alone in what I experienced. Loneliness is a defining characteristic of addiction, but through our stories, we develop common bonds with other people.

I hope my story gives a bit of that to you.

So, *what was it like?*

I grew up in the 1980s in a small area of Southern California called Jurupa Valley, just a few miles outside Riverside. It was a rural town with many dairy farms (now replaced with tract homes), paved and dirt roads (I grew up on a dirt one), and a lot of horses (my parents had two).

My father was a truck driver, while my mother worked at the nearby college in a role that was a mixture of data entry and student worker supervision. They had two sons within a year and a half of each other; I was the youngest of them. My dad was a constantly swearing, chain-smoking alcoholic. My mother is a never swearing, never drinking or smoking, highly devout Christian.

It is safe to say they did not have a good marriage.

My father was never around, working six days a week. And the one day he had off (Sundays) was spent drinking beer and watching television.

As a family, we did nothing together, were isolated from extended family (unless it was a special holiday), and when my father would have vacation time, he would spend days on end getting drunk. My mother did her best to protect us from my father's drunken verbal abuse when he had too much. But she could only do her best, and it was not always possible to do so.

My first addiction would be hard for people to see. I was so paranoid (early signs of anxiety issues) about becoming like my father that I obsessed over my performance in school. I always had to get the best grades so I would not end up like him and the struggles I had seen him going through with his work. As I entered high school, I was so obsessed with doing good in school that I would constantly strive for perfection in my schoolwork. I never really went out with friends or did anything on weekends. I was at the top of my class and needed to maintain that at all costs.

School was my life.

At around the age of sixteen, drugs would first enter my life. A childhood friend of mine moved back to the area and came by my house (since we had never moved) to say hello. He ended up giving me the first joint that I would ever smoke. All the anxiety and obsession with being that perfect kid disappeared with that joint, and for the first time, I could remember feeling relaxed without a care in the world.

I finally felt peace of mind (although it had been drug-induced).

Spending more time with him, I got introduced to new friends and immersed myself in the 1990s punk scene with backyard parties and local shows almost every weekend. And this would be when drinking would enter my life. However, drinking and smoking would mainly remain a weekend activity for me during these years. I never thought badly of the drinking and drugs I was consuming (I had experimented with other types) because it did not affect my school. I would graduate from high school fourth in my class and get accepted to the local college to study conservation biology. Since I stayed local, I could still spend time with all my friends and keep up the same drinking and drug use patterns, although marijuana was creeping into daily use.

College was more difficult, but I still did quite well in classes, so I thought nothing of what I was doing. However, I would feel more of my mental disorder in these years. I can look back and notice moments of being manic, depressed, and even my first experiences of dissociation. I felt that every day was not real, seeing the world as if I was watching a television show (I still struggle with this feeling constantly). At the end of my undergraduate years, I would be accepted into a prestigious marine biology laboratory in Long Beach and, for the first time, move away from home to be alone in the world. I would struggle more here than ever in school since I was doing something I had never tried before since I grew up nowhere near the ocean.

When I look back at my graduate school years with the eyes of recovery, I can now see that this is where signs of my addiction showed through in my life. Being away from home and alone, codependency emerged. I met a woman, moved in with her within three months, and married her six months later. My weed smoking became a daily activity. I drank more often and developed a nasty cocaine habit for a while. Then, of course, I quit this cocaine addiction by smoking more weed and drinking because I do not have a problem with addiction as long as I drink and smoke.

Right?

These addictions impacted my life as my graduate research went nowhere (because I was hardly in the lab), and I ran out of my welcome at the school. But my wife at the time had become pregnant, so I thought it was all for the better. I didn't need to graduate school; I had to find a career.

We would move back to my parent's house so that I could get started on a career while we waited for the baby to be born. My dad had developed cancer since I moved away and quit drinking because of this, making him more tolerable to be around. However, he was getting to the final stages, so I had to watch him deteriorate as cancer consumed him. An image forever burned in my mind was seeing this powerful man I always had feared growing up, crawling on his knees to make it to the bathroom and me having to pick up his frail body to bring him there.

In the same year, I would become a father to an amazing daughter and lose mine.

The career I would eventually choose would be that of a high school science teacher. It was the easiest and fastest one for someone with a science degree to get into since there is always a high demand. It was something that came naturally to me.

I was a good teacher.

My students did well, I was well-liked, and the administration thought highly of me.

But I was not a "good" teacher.

I jokingly had a rotten apple tattooed on my arm. I had the apple since it is associated with teachers, but it was rotten because I always noted that I was rotten inside. I never paid attention to what I was telling myself. I often showed up to teach high on weed or hungover from the night before. Pick any day, and it was one or the other or both.

All this occurred around the Great Recession when schools had to lay off teachers due to budget cutbacks. So, I would hop around from school to school for a few years before I ended up in the Los Angeles area and living downtown, an area fueled by alcohol and drugs, although I mainly drank and smoked weed.

Every night and all weekends now.

My marriage declined to a total collapse. I was a liar and a cheater while becoming more verbally abusive. I had become my father at his worst and surpassed him toward deeper depths. I would end up pushing my wife to where she couldn't handle it any longer. She would take my daughter and leave me.

Probably the best decision of her life.

Now on my own, I was free to be overtaken by my inner demons and begin my downward spiral. One that would last nearly five years. I look back on a five-year blur and think just simply...wow.

Ready for a plunging ride?

I drank daily. I drank before work and as soon as the school day ended. Eventually, I had to drink at work since my hands were shaking so badly; I needed alcohol in my system to write straight on the board. On the way to work, I side-swiped a vehicle while drunk and got my first drunk driving conviction. I took time off work and entered my first outpatient rehab with reservations in my mind. Went back to work. I started drinking again because I told myself I had it under control. Right back to where I was getting drunk during the school day. I got caught and was forced to resign. Moved in with my mom. Continued to drink. Got kicked out of her house for being drunk and her being fed up. At this point, I was homeless with only a bag of clothes to my name. I lived in motel rooms with the bit of money I had. A friend let me stay at his place. He got me another teaching job. I rebuilt a life. Went back to drinking. Went back to being drunk in the classroom and acting out. Got caught. Fired. Became suicidal. Ended up in a mental hospital. They finally diagnosed me with bipolar disorder, but the meds were wrong. Went to a dual diagnosis outpatient rehab. Convinced myself I just needed to smoke weed, and I would be fine. Weed was not enough, so I would go back to drinking. Had my credential stripped away from me. Could only find warehouse work. Got fired once again for being drunk on the job.

Whew!

I believe that brings me to the *what happened* part of my story.

Before my DUI, I had dated a woman when I was still living in downtown Los Angeles. She had stayed by my side pretty much throughout all the madness of that last paragraph. We were living together in a house in the mountains. She worked hard to support us since I could not hold a job. And I was constantly letting her down by drinking behind her back, although any of us who have dealt with addiction know that they know. It is never truly behind their back.

And she knew.

April 18th, 2018.

I was back to drinking regularly. Jobless. Having money problems. Medicated improperly. And becoming suicidal again.

I had an appointment with a psychiatrist that day. I picked up alcohol on my drive down the mountains and drank to my appointment. The waiting room took too long, so I got fed up and stormed out. I would drink in my car for a while before deciding to return home. Although I was thinking of just ending my life again. Completely drunk, as I drove up the mountain's winding roads, I collided with a large rock on the side of the road.

While changing the tire, a highway patrol vehicle would pull up to check on me. The officers could smell the alcohol. And the evidence was sitting in the car as well. With a DUI on my record already, they knew to check me.

My second DUI.

They towed away my car. I was brought to the county jail and held in the intake area for the rest of the day. When I was released in the morning, like any good alcoholic, I went down to the nearest place where I could buy alcohol and bought a case of beer. I sat in an empty grass field and just drank.

My girlfriend could not pick me up since they had towed the car. Besides, she did not want to talk to me, anyway. She was moving out and I had no home to return to. My mother wanted no part of my life. My brother washed his hands of me years ago, and I had long lost all my friends.

I had nobody and nothing.

I sat in that field drinking as I watched the cars on the freeway pass. All I could think about was how all those driving had somewhere to go. They probably had jobs. A home. Family. Friends. And I had none of that. One part of Stoicism that builds appreciation in life is for you to think of losing everything you have. So, when frustration comes into my life these days, or I find myself without gratitude, I think of this moment and realize that my life could be that way again.

This was the moment I was done.

I guess you could call it my Step 1 if you are a step person.

I would end up checking myself into a mental hospital close to where I was. I would spend two weeks there leveling out and requesting them to find me an inpatient rehab this time. I would end up at an all-men's rehab, where I would spend nearly 100 days. For the first time since that first joint I had smoked all those years ago, I finally felt sober. They would give me a different group of meds that would actually work this time for my bipolar condition. I would work on myself in a place I could not leave.

Then came my court date for my second DUI, and let's say the judge was not happy. They charged me with DUI alcohol, DUI psychiatric medicines, DUI alcohol and psychiatric medicines, and they even got me for hitting the rock. I would be immediately remanded into custody to spend 30 days in the county. Sobering up and working on yourself and then having to spend 30 days in county jail for something you did drunk is a further reminder of how bad it was.

When I was released, I moved to an all-men's sober living to keep working on my sobriety. And a little over three years later, I am still here writing this book for you.

Now the last part...*what it is like now.*

For all of us that have had some time in recovery, we know that just stopping already improves your life, as long as you do not transfer your addictions to something else. For example, I have been able to rebuild relationships in my life. It took some time, but they have improved immensely.

Missing much of my daughter's life through my past addictions means I must lose no more time in my present recovery. She is just starting her teens, so I now have to deal with having a teenager. We are growing closer as I see and talk to her more. I have taken up some of her interests, so we can have more to discuss, and she has begun to text me...which is an enormous accomplishment to achieve with a teenager.

I have communicated better with my ex-wife, and we no longer fight or argue. My relationship with my mother is closer than ever, and I have been able to build back one with my brother. I even had a few friends come back into my life.

I rebuilt my relationship with my girlfriend as we are approaching seven years together while writing this book. She has seen me at my worst, and the only thing I can do is give her my best. She deserves it. Our relationship has hit a new level and a depth that never existed. I sometimes ask her what kept her around and why she returned. She tells me she knew I was a good person, but I was just lost. How could you not love someone who says something like that to you?

After years of turmoil, my journey to sobriety began in a step program during my time at the rehab facility. Subsequently, the sober living environment I now reside in incorporates meetings on-site, mandatory for all residents. These initial steps provided me with the essential grounding and momentum in my recovery journey. Seeking a different perspective, I also explored Dharma Recovery, a Buddhist program, which offered me valuable insights into addiction and recovery.

However, it was through embracing Stoicism that my life witnessed the most profound transformations. Being an all-encompassing philosophy, Stoicism transcends mere theoretical contemplation; it becomes a way of life. It has changed my entire view of the world and how I live daily. In the second part of this book, you will find more of my story and how Stoicism has become a part of it.

I guess this means to be continued for *what it is like now...*

The Enchiridion:
Expanded for a Stoic Recovery

Some Quick Notes on Part Two

B efore I get into the central part of this book, I wanted to give some quick notes on what to expect ahead. The *Enchiridion* was a short manual with fifty-three chapters Arrian had compiled as notes from Epictetus's lectures. They number the chapters in the original work. I have added titles underneath each of the chapter numbers. The titles are my own, and I have written them to give you a preview of what to expect. Think of them as the primary point Epictetus touches on within the chapter.

In part one, I described the Four Cardinal Virtues of Stoicism (wisdom, justice, courage, and temperance) and how they intertwine in pursuit of excellence. Underneath each title, I will give the virtues focused on in that chapter. If you find this philosophy to be one you want to implement, this should allow you to see what virtue you will develop through that chapter.

For each chapter, I will present you with what Epictetus says. Then I will expand upon what he is discussing to give you a deeper understanding of how it relates to Stoicism, addiction, recovery, and life. Some of his chapters are longer, so I will break them into several parts.

Thomas Wentworth Higginson wrote the translation I chose in 1865, meaning the language can seem dated in some chapters. My discussions should help to clarify any difficulties. I selected this edition since it is in the public domain, which means you can find it online for free if you want to download just the *Enchiridion* alone for your possession.

Enjoy the journey.

CHAPTER 1

The Serenity Prayer
(Temperance, Wisdom)

There are things which are within our power, and there are things which are beyond our power. Within our power are opinion, aim, desire, aversion, and, in one word, whatever affairs are our own. Beyond our power are body, property, reputation, office, and, in one word, whatever are not properly our own affairs. – Chapter 1, Epictetus' Enchiridion.

I always find it so interesting to attend meetings and listen to the audience during the Serenity Prayer. It becomes this kind of entity we all know and have memorized by heart. But we say it so many times that I think for some of us, we can lose sight of the wisdom that it contains. As I said in the book's first part, the Stoics practiced the Serenity Prayer thousands of years before being written. It is the foundational logic referenced throughout the rest of this book. I remember communicating with one of the modern Stoics once, who shared an anecdote about speaking to an individual in recovery from addiction who was practicing Stoicism, and he described it as the Serenity Prayer on steroids.

In Stoicism, it is not so much about the things that we can or cannot change; it is about the things we have control (power) over and the things that we do not. We have no control over the things that we neither have the ability nor power to change. Therefore, it is best to focus your time on that over which you have control and learn to accept the rest. Living your life this way will allow you to make the most of it. We waste so much time getting angry, worrying, or stressing over things we cannot do anything about while neglecting what we can change.

The first thing that Epictetus says that we do not control is our own body. It is funny to think that something we see as belonging to us is not actually under our control. Although when you think about it, it should make sense. We do not decide our genetic makeup, and even our parents have no say in this; random events at the cellular level determine the genes that become the blueprints for the body that we use to navigate life. We cannot choose our height, metabolic processes that determine weight, the color of our skin, eyes, hair, and even a psychiatric condition (I must accept that I am bipolar). Illness is beyond our control, and harm once it has occurred. And yes, for those in recovery, we cannot control our addictions or the consequences of substance use. This is because it alters the very functioning of our brains significantly.

The idea that we have no control over the things we own or possess was Epictetus' way of saying that even though it might be yours today, it can be gone tomorrow. How many of us have hit those hard bottoms where we lost everything?—our homes, relationships, jobs, and possessions. Like sand flows through our fingers, everything

STOIC GUIDEBOOK FOR RECOVERY

vanishes through the grips of addiction. What once might have been our own is lost from our possessive grasp.

And it is not only addiction that could be the cause of this. How many things have you owned that became lost to you through it becoming broken or stolen? How many jobs have ended because your employer did not need your work or wanted to find someone else? How many relationships have ended because the person you were with wanted to see someone else? Life is ephemeral and what we possess throughout our existence is even more so.

Reputation can be defined as recognition by other people of some characteristic or ability. You can see in the definition that it is something given to us by others. How you will be viewed by the people in your life will be determined by them. Therefore, it is up to them whether they will see you with a positive or negative view. Epictetus understood this well, as he witnessed his reputation change depending on which emperor was in power. Now, you can try to influence your reputation by your actions and interactions with others. But in the end, it is up to that other person to decide how they will perceive you.

The destructive grasp of addiction can sometimes damage the reputation we bring into recovery. And we might sometimes wonder why the people we care about in life do not see everything we are doing to improve ourselves. However, it is not and will never be in our power to decide how they view us. In some cases, our years of addictive behavior may have shaped negative opinions in the minds of those around us. It is unrealistic to expect them to instantly forget about the years of negative impressions we have chiseled into their minds just because we have now decided to make a change. Creating a new impression takes time, and there is a possibility that it may never happen, especially if we have caused significant harm. The quicker we understand this, the faster we can release ourselves from the negative feelings we punish ourselves with over how others might see us.

"'Station in life,' then, can be changed from that of a dignified and competent gentleman of culture to that of a panic-stricken, sobbing, self-loathing wreck in a matter of minutes. So what? To live under the false pretense that you will forever have control of your station in life is to ride for a fall; you're asking for disappointment." – James Bond Stockdale, Courage Under Fire, pg. 9.

Your station in life or the office you hold is your social position. First, we do not choose the social class we are born into; it is given to us by our parents (like how Epictetus was born into slavery). Then, as James Stockdale discovered, it can change within an instant. He went from being a free man to a prisoner of war within seconds as they shot his fighter jet down during the Vietnam War. It was not a choice he made; it was because of actions outside his control. Indeed, even Epictetus had to rely on someone else—the man who owned him—to grant him his freedom from slavery in order to change his station in life.

However, the Stoics do not say you cannot change your station in life. In fact, many of the goals we can lay out for ourselves are ways to improve the conditions we live in and move up the social ladder. You can easily find examples of people who started life in poverty to end life in luxury. But if you look at these examples deeply, you will be able to discover that things outside of that person's control had to happen for this to occur. Because as easily as you can find these stories of rags to riches, you can find other stories of people who tried to do the same thing. It is just that the outside forces did not work in their favor, so nothing came of it.

With all these things out of our control, what is within it?

The reality...

Very little.

Here it becomes crucial to recognize that while external circumstances may present challenges, we still have agency over our actions and can exert control over our own lives, even in the face of adversity. We control any opinions we form, our life pursuits, and what we choose to desire and avoid. We control the actions we commit to at any moment. For example, the option to drink or use is now lost to us, but as we learn in recovery, we decide what to do (one day at a time) to keep us on our path to sobriety.

Stoicism teaches people how to make the most out of the things they control in life to become their best version.

Now, the things within our power are by nature free, unrestricted, unhindered; but those beyond our power are weak, dependent, restricted, alien. Remember that if you attribute freedom to things by nature dependent, and take what belongs to others for your own, you will be hindered, you will lament, you will be disturbed, you will find fault both with gods and men. But if you take for your own only that which is your own, and view what belongs to others just as it really is, then no one will ever compel you, no one will restrict you, you will find fault with no one, you will accuse no one, you will do nothing against your will; no one will hurt you, you will not have an enemy, nor will you suffer any harm. – Chapter 1, Epictetus' Enchiridion.

DEREK CASTLEMAN & EPICTETUS

The fact that Epictetus spent a part of his life enslaved gave him an interesting perspective on what a person truly owns. In this second part of the chapter, he describes how the things we have in our control belong to us. There are no rules or restrictions on them; nothing can impede them, and nobody can take them away.

Your opinions, what you choose to desire, pursue, or avoid, and the actions you will take (someone can tell you what to do, but it is your choice if you will do it), belong to you and only you. The things you do not control are not free to you, have restrictions, and belong to someone else.

Epictetus then follows this up with a warning.

If a person claims the things that do not belong to them as belonging to them, they will find themselves unable to attain the freedom they desire. Instead, this person will discover themselves suffering in sorrow, dealing with negative emotions, and blaming God or other people for their life problems.

This person will be filled with anger...resentment...or both.

Anger and resentment are dangerous for recovery. They can become a straightforward path right back into our addiction.

You are trying to control the uncontrollable.

To illustrate this point, let's return to the concept of the reputation that we do not own. Now it is completely in our control to decide how we view ourselves. Self-esteem is literally defined as how we perceive and value ourselves, which is why it is in our control. But if we want to control our reputation, we are setting ourselves up for failure and negative emotions. We may want the people in our lives to think positively of us now that we are in recovery, but we have no right to expect this to happen. It belongs to them. And the more that we concern ourselves with our reputation and try to control it in our favor, the more emotional damage we are setting ourselves up for if it does not work out the way we want.

Did you lose a job, a relationship, where you lived, or something you owned and then blame someone else for causing it? Did someone say something you did not like or do something you disapproved of? In this part, Epictetus discussed that these things never belonged to you, and the problem is that you thought they were owed to you. You wanted things to be how you wanted them to be, and that did not happen.

Seize the things in your life that you own and learn to let go of the rest. And if you can, you will no longer blame anyone else and be free from resentment. You will never again do anything that you choose not to. Nobody can hurt you any longer, and you will have no more enemies. It is through understanding and accepting these things that we can find ourselves on the path to a life in which we are satisfied with ourselves.

———

Aiming therefore at such great things, remember that you must not allow yourself any inclination, however slight, towards the attainment of the others; but that you must entirely quit some of them, and for the present postpone the rest. But if you would have these, and possess power and wealth likewise, you may miss the latter in seeking the former; and you will certainly fail of that by which alone happiness and freedom are procured. – Chapter 1, Epictetus' Enchiridion.

———

There is more to life than money and power.

Those of us in recovery know this well.

To be alive to see the morning sun with sober eyes is a priceless blessing. But sadly, for some of us, with each passing morning, we can find diminishing value in witnessing that sight. The ache and urge to get all the things we may have lost through our addictions can begin to pulsate and writhe through our veins. It becomes a growing din within our minds getting louder and louder with each passing day.

I have given into that screaming din.

During my first bottom, I experienced homelessness for the first time. And after a couple of months of sobriety, I focused on getting back all the things I had lost—the job, house, car, etc.

Which I did.

To lose them all again was to experience a bottom even worse than before. I forgot I needed to work on myself; that was more critical. I know I am not the only one to discover this. Throughout my recovery, I have heard stories from many people who had multiple relapses on their journey toward sobriety as they lost sight of maintaining focus on what was important.

This section of the chapter is Epictetus's way of saying, "Easy does it." We must take our time in recovery. We need to work on ourselves and strengthen who we are first. There is nothing wrong with money or power. The Stoics Seneca and Marcus Aurelius (the emperor) were quite wealthy. However, they both were okay with giving them up. Seneca offered his wealth to the emperor he worked for when he retired (although he got to keep it), and Marcus Aurelius left the palace life behind to be on the war front.

Money and power are called preferred indifferents to the Stoics. Would a person prefer them? Who wouldn't? But we must learn to be indifferent to them simultaneously because they lie within that realm of the things outside our control.

Aim for the great things in life; your goal should be working on yourself and who you are. Pursuing certain aspects of life (like getting back things you have lost) might have to be delayed. Remember, true happiness and freedom emanate from your inner being, not wealth and power. Once you have paid attention to what matters most, there is always time for the rest.

Seek at once, therefore, to be able to say to every unpleasing semblance, "You are but a semblance and by no means the real thing." And then examine it by those rules which you have; and first and chiefly, by this: whether it concerns the things which are within our own power, or those which are not; and if it concerns anything beyond our power, be prepared to say that it is nothing to you. – Chapter 1, Epictetus' Enchiridion.

How can you implement the ideas you learned about in this chapter?

How can you live the Serenity Prayer to its fullest?

Whenever you must confront something in life, whether good or bad, first, take a breath and tell yourself that even though it might look a certain way, it is just how it looks. Remember, your opinion is something that you own and control.

After you have taken your breath, your moment, that brief pause you need so that you do not instantly react or overreact to anything and everything that happens, use the rules given earlier in this chapter.

Ask yourself if this is something that is in your control or not. If it is, then it is something that you should be concerned about since you can do something. However, if something is out of your control, shrug it off because why should you be bothered or worried about something you cannot do anything about?

It may be challenging to do this at first (it was for me), but over time you get more and more used to it.

In the end, this chapter was the Stoic equivalent of the Serenity Prayer. We need to accept the things we cannot change (do not have any control over) and have the courage to change the things we can (what we have control over). The final thing to point out is that this is under the category of wisdom regarding Stoic virtues. And if you notice, the Serenity Prayer asks for the wisdom to see the difference between the things we cannot change and those we can.

God grant me the serenity
to accept the things I cannot change;
courage to change the things I can;
and wisdom to know the difference.
– The Serenity Prayer

CHAPTER 2

The Dangers of Desire and Aversion
(Temperance, Wisdom)

Remember that desire demands the attainment of that of which you are desirous; and aversion demands the avoidance of that to which you are averse; that he who fails of the object of his desires is disappointed; and he who incurs the object of his aversion is wretched. – Chapter 2, Epictetus' Enchiridion.

In the first chapter, I briefly discussed that what we choose to desire and what we choose to oppose (averse) is within our control. So, the best way to think of this chapter is simply this: choose wisely, because it is how we choose these things that will determine the potential impact they can have on our emotions. Consequences can be completely avoidable if we select the right things to desire and oppose.

When we select to follow the path of desire, we promise ourselves that it is our goal to get what we seek. When we choose what we oppose (aversion), we pledge to ourselves what we will choose to avoid. For example, in recovery, we desire sobriety and promise to do whatever it takes to maintain it. However, we also decide that we oppose what we are addicted to (alcohol, drugs, gambling, sex, etc.), and we promise ourselves to avoid them. But what happens if we do not get what we desire or experience what we tried to avoid?

The worst thing about a relapse is getting hit with both sides. Not only do you do what you want to avoid (your addiction), you lose what you had desired (your sobriety). During my relapses, I would find myself drinking once again even though I was no longer getting any pleasure from it. Those days of drinking for enjoyment were long lost in the days of a past that I would never be able to return to. I would be in this downward spiral of emotions, as I was disappointed to find that I was doing what I said I would not do and losing the sobriety I truly wanted. This disappointment would lead to a deep depression and, eventually, suicidal thoughts.

The Stoics realized that the problem with what we choose to desire and avoid could be the devastating effects on our emotions if we do not achieve them. And it is when we become caught in negative emotions that we make poor decisions (the suicidal thoughts I was having in my relapses). Therefore, we need to think wisely about what we choose to desire and oppose to maintain a healthy mental state.

If you shun only those undesirable things which you can control, you will never incur anything which you shun; but if you shun sickness, or death, or poverty, you will run the risk of wretchedness. Remove the habit of aversion from all things that are not within our power, and apply it to things undesirable, which are within our power. – Chapter 2, Epictetus' Enchiridion.

Epictetus discusses we need never oppose or be averse to things that are not in our control. Luckily for us, with the right help and proper actions, avoiding our addictions is something that we have in our possession. However, we cannot choose things like sickness, death, or poverty as what we will oppose because we have no power to avoid them. Yes, we may not like them or want them to happen to us, but it is not like we can guarantee them to be completely avoidable.

How many times have you been sick in your life? Of all those times you have been ill, how many times did you ask for it to happen? Sickness is unavoidable; it will happen to everyone in life. The pandemic taught us we could take all the precautions to avoid getting sick (social distancing, wearing a mask, vaccination, etc.), yet there was no guarantee that it would not happen.

Death is also inevitable, the end of ourselves and everyone we know. It is the one guarantee that all living creatures are promised to experience the moment they are born. Therefore, we need to live a life where we accept death's possibility daily to be ready for when it comes to us and our loved ones.

Some people want a life of poverty; the Cynics, discussed in this book's first part, would feel fine living that way. But for most of us, this would not be something we would openly want. Yet, it is not something you can choose to avoid. Search online, and you can find many examples of people who amassed large amounts of wealth (athletes, lottery winners, musicians, businesspeople, etc.) but saw all the money disappearing through poor decisions or things simply out of their control.

The problem with choosing things outside your power to avoid is that you could set yourself up for failure. For example, what will happen if sickness, death, or poverty visits your life unexpectedly? You tried everything possible to avoid it but could not since it was out of your power. Suddenly, you are vulnerable and hit with negative emotions such as depression, anger, anxiety, etc., because you find yourself dealing with what you were trying your hardest to avoid. And for those in recovery, this puts us on shaky ground. How many stories of relapse have you heard that followed events of death, job loss, or a diagnosis of an illness? However, by genuinely understanding and accepting the limitations of our control, we gain the opportunity to navigate these unavoidable challenges with greater resilience. Embracing the Stoic principle of accepting the uncontrollable aspects of life allows us to transcend deep feelings of grief and disappointment should they arise, granting us a better chance to maintain our sobriety.

Therefore, rather than trying to avoid anything you do not have control over, focus on what you do. Choose to oppose things that do not align with who you want to be. For example, do you want to be an honest person? Then make telling lies what you choose to avoid. Do you want to be even-tempered? Then choose to oppose getting angry or frustrated and annoyed. Do you want to be a good parent, sibling, or friend? What actions should you avoid that will keep you from serving these roles? These things are in your power to prevent, and focusing on them rather than what you do not have control over allows you to use your time more effectively while leading to better peace of mind.

But for the present altogether restrain desire; for if you desire any of the things not within our own power, you must necessarily be disappointed; and you are not yet secure of those which are within our power, and so are legitimate objects of desire. Where it is practically necessary for you to pursue or avoid anything, do even this with discretion, and gentleness, and moderation. – Chapter 2, Epictetus' Enchiridion.

For the last part of this chapter, Epictetus says that the most immediate thing we need to do is restrain our desire. First, ask someone what they want to avoid in life. Then ask them what they want. They will probably be able to quickly and more easily answer the things they want. People are filled with desires. It is a powerful force within all of us. And the Stoics realized that this force was insatiable. Give someone everything they want, and they will have another list of even more in a short amount of time.

> *"The philosophies were therapies, intended to provide a cure for anguish, and to bring freedom and self-mastery, and their goal was to allow people to free themselves from the past and the future, so they could live within the present." – Pierre Hadot, Philosophy as a Way of Life, pgs. 221-222.*

The issue with desire is easily discoverable through the definition of the word alone. To desire is to wish or want for something strongly. What this implies is that it is something that exists in the future and is not within your grasp in the present. Stoicism, as a philosophy, focuses our lives on the present moment, not the future. The two reasons for this are:

1. The present moment is the only thing we have in our lives.
2. The future is unknown, with many possibilities that could happen.

Stoics emphasize an approach in which you have goals to achieve, but you work towards them, understanding that there is a possibility they could not happen because of unforeseen events. However, this does not mean that you do not work as hard as you can; many Ancient Stoics (and some modern ones) achieved great things in life. It is just another way to protect yourself from negative emotions if things do not work out the way you want them.

Staying in a sober living home for so long has given me deep insight into why this is so important. Desires are plentiful in a sober living. Have any conversation with a resident, and you will discover all the wants they seek in their sobriety that were ripped away from them through their addictions.

Desires to get back to work.

Desires to have a place of their own again.

Desires to reconcile addiction-ravaged relationships.

However, the destruction of addiction becomes evident in any resume submitted for a job, which makes employment difficult to find. Without employment, it makes it more difficult to attain the money needed to move out. And relationships are rarely restored quickly when years of letdowns, abandonment, or abuse have taken their toll on them.

You can genuinely hear the frustration in these conversations about not getting what they want fast enough. Let's face it, the addicts in us love instant gratification. But no matter how often you tell them to focus on themselves and give it some time, a few always give in to the negative emotions.

Stay enough time in a sober living, and you will witness multiple relapses.

Stay long enough, and you will have to deal with some deaths.

You can see this idea of focusing on yourself in what Epictetus says. He says to hold off on desires until you grow enough in the new life you are trying to live. You need to understand what truly matters in life to actually desire correctly. Work towards a virtuous life, grow deeper insight into yourself, and with enough time, you will understand what to choose to avoid correctly and what is worth desiring in the world.

"The Master said, 'The superior man, in the world, does not set his mind either for anything, or against anything; what is right he will follow.'" – Confucius, The Analects, 4.10.

CHAPTER 3

Preparing for Loss
(Temperance, Wisdom)

With regard to whatever objects either delight the mind or contribute to use or are tenderly beloved, remind yourself of what nature they are, beginning with the merest trifles: if you have a favorite cup, that it is but a cup of which you are fond of—for thus, if it is broken, you can bear it; if you embrace your child or your wife, that you embrace a mortal—and thus, if either of them dies, you can bear it. – Chapter 3, Epictetus' Enchiridion.

L oss is inevitable. Out of our control. Something we cannot oppose. Something we must learn to accept. And loss can come to us in many ways. It can be from the death of a loved one, separation or divorce, loss of employment, moving away, or even giving up something that matters (HealthDirect Australia n.d.). It is most often associated with feelings of grief that can vary from person to person in expression. People can express grief through sadness, shock, denial, anger, guilt, and even blame.

It is difficult for anyone to deal with, addict or not.

For those who suffer from addiction, handling feelings of grief is essential. Studies have shown a link between bereavement and hazardous alcohol consumption. People with over two years of grief are twice as likely to have an alcohol use disorder (American Addiction Centers, 2022). While people who suffer from complicated grief (around 10-20% of bereaved individuals) are highly vulnerable because of patterns in the brain that relate memories of loved ones to the addiction centers. The drug of choice becomes a way in which we try to drown out the feelings that we are experiencing. Handling loss becomes vital to recovery because not only could it have been one cause of your addiction, but it could also put you in danger of relapse.

The things that we have control over are those that cannot be taken away. Since loss is literally about something that is taken away, it lies in the realm of the uncontrollable. Nevertheless, the Stoics felt that there must be something we could do to mentally prepare ourselves for the possibility of losing things we care for.

In this chapter, Epictetus introduces the Stoic concept of premeditatio malorum (pre-meditation of evils), sometimes referred to as negative visualization. The basic idea is that, occasionally, you take a few moments to think about the bad things that could happen. Bad things like loss. Imagine the things you have in your life and what would happen if they were gone. It prepares the mind to cope with adversity and face trials in life by imagining various difficulties, reversals of fortune, sufferings, and even death (Robertson 2020, pg. 179).

The method of negative visualization can have two potentially positive effects.

First, you can hopefully be better prepared when loss comes into your life since you have been working out your mind to prepare for it. Not that grief will be gone, but it may not be as profoundly impactful or of long duration, which is good for us since, as pointed out above, long periods of grief increase the possibility of giving into the addiction.

The second benefit of this is the development of gratitude. Often, when we lose things in life, we realize we have taken them for granted. You can become grateful for what you have right now in life by thinking about how it would be if they were gone. It reminds me of when I spent time in county for my second DUI. I wasn't even in there long, only thirty days. However, this came after ninety days in a completely isolated in-patient rehab and several weeks in a mental hospital before it (this was my last bottom). I left county with a new understanding of gratitude. Being able to walk outdoors, get fresh air, feel the sun, and go wherever I want when I want. Spending time with my loved ones, being able to call them anytime I want and talk to them however long I wanted to. Showering without other guys walking by just a few feet away, a comfortable bed, watching whatever I want on TV, eating a delicious meal, actually eating whenever I want to eat. I took all these things in life for granted; I did not realize how special they were until they were taken away.

Imagining loss makes you grateful for the life you have.

Epictetus explains how to practice and strengthen this ability of negative visualization in this chapter. First, start with the simple things in life. For example, if you have that favorite cup or coffee mug, tell yourself that it is just a cup or mug, and life isn't over if it breaks. Next, imagine yourself losing that cup. What would you do?

Your computer is just a computer. Your cell phone is just a phone. Your TV is just a TV. All these replaceable items will eventually break; they will not last forever. Then move this mental practice onto bigger things. Your car is just a car. You have probably had multiple cars in your life by now. Your job is just a job. You have probably had other jobs that you have either lost or quit and could get another one. The main thing to do is spend some time imagining what you would do if you lost these things. How will you recover from that? But as you imagine losing all these things in life, take a moment and have gratitude over the fact they are not gone and are with you today.

Epictetus finishes this chapter by telling you to move to the ultimate level and remind yourself that the loved ones in your life are all mortal and that death awaits all of them. You need to mentally prepare yourself for the possibility of their death and how you will cope with it. And yes, even the death of your child is a possibility that you must prepare for.

By 60 years old, 9% of Americans have experienced the death of a child, which increases to 15% by 70 (Umberson 2017). My grandparents experienced the death of both sons and a grandchild (my uncle's only one) during their lifetime. A child's death can increase a parent's mortality risk. One study found that mothers have a 326% increased chance of dying within the first two years of the death of a child (Baer 2016). Therefore, we must prepare for an event like this, not only for our sobriety but also for its devastating impact on health and the possibility of our own death. Grief will still be there, but we can have the chance to lessen its effect by considering the possibility of it occurring.

There is also the issue of taking our loved ones for granted. Some of us have experienced the destruction of our relationships during our addictions. Some of us may have even taken time for granted with our children during our addictions. I can remember times when I canceled plans with my daughter because getting drunk was a higher priority to me than spending time with her. And through my addictions, I have missed out on a good portion of her younger years that I can never get back. And if she had somehow met an untimely death during those years, I would have had to live with the knowledge that I missed out on experiencing my daughter's life.

In his book, *A Guide to the Good Life*, William Irvine discusses how negative visualization can help improve our time with our loved ones. He discusses a scenario of two fathers. One father contemplates the death of his child. Another father does not want to think gloomy thoughts and assumes his child will outlive him and always be around (Irvine 2009, pg.69).

How will the interactions between these two fathers and their children differ?

One pictures this day as a blessing and could be the last one with his child. The other father sees an indefinite future and has a chance of another day. How would these two fathers differ in their interactions with their children on any given day based on the different perspectives they take? And which one might have more regrets over things left unsaid or undone if the child passes away?

I have implemented negative visualization in my life regarding my teenage daughter, which has transformed our relationship. Where we once spent a lot of time on our cell phones around each other doing our own thing, the time spent doing that has dramatically decreased. I let her control the radio in the car so that we can listen to her music and I can learn about what she likes about it. We play a massive amount of board games together. I constantly start conversations about her life and what is going on. I watch all the movies and shows she likes, so we can talk about characters and storylines. I am always looking for new activities we can do for quality time together. It has gotten so good that where she used to never text me before when we were apart (she is a teenager, after all), she now starts text conversations with me about the things we discuss. Much of this came from thinking to myself, what if this was my last day with her? How would I want it to be spent?

And even though my addictions took years of time with her away. I have no regrets. I am actually grateful. Because I have my daughter in my present. Something could have happened to her that would have taken her away so that I would not have the moments I have now. Rather than dwell in the moment on what was lost, I choose to live in the present with what I gained.

Loss impacts everyone, both addicts and non-addicts. However, for us who have suffered from addiction and are in recovery, we need to find healthy ways to prepare and deal with it to maintain our sobriety. We have no control over what we will lose in life, but we have control over how we will handle it. Only if we have thought through the scenarios will we have given ourselves practice for the real thing. Negative visualization will not eliminate all grief, but it can reduce the impact of it somewhat while building a higher sense of gratitude for the life you are living today.

Today can be the best day of your life if you step back and see all you have.

"I saw grief drinking a cup of sorrow and called out, 'It tastes sweet, does it not?' 'You've caught me,' grief answered, 'and you've ruined my business. How can I sell sorrow, when you know it's a blessing?'" – Rumi

CHAPTER 4

Expect the Expected
(Temperance)

When you set about any action, remind yourself of what nature the action is. If you are going to bathe, represent to yourself the incidents usual in the bath—some persons pouring out, others pushing in, others scolding, others pilfering. And thus you will more safely go about this action if you say to yourself, "I will now go to bathe and keep my own will in harmony with nature." And so with regard to every other action. For thus, if any impediment arises in bathing, you will be able to say, "It was not only to bathe that I desired, but to keep my will in harmony with nature; and I shall not keep it thus if I am out of humor at things that happen." – Chapter 4, Epictetus' Enchiridion.

Stoicism emphasizes the self-control of emotions because of the choices we make when we do not have control over them. Usually irrational choices. Think of all the times you made the wrong decision when you did not have control over your emotions. One of the harshest realizations of sobriety is facing the massive destruction we have wrought on our lives through decisions we made under the influence when our self-control was minimized. As you have seen in the last few chapters, Epictetus was advising on ways to avoid frustration and disappointment and prepare ourselves for handling grief. In this chapter, he focuses on how we can maintain a level head in any situation we find ourselves in. Keeping a level head in different situations is crucial to a healthy recovery since stress commonly triggers relapse (Northstar Transitions 2020). And one cause of stress is when unexpected events occur in life.

It is common to hear the saying to "expect the unexpected," but Stoics feel it is more helpful to live by 'expecting the expected.'

In the example you read above, you can see how Epictetus discusses how to prepare for going to a bathhouse to take a bath (something that would have been common while he lived). He reminds himself of what he should expect from the other people around him when going to the bathhouse and that he wants to keep his mind comfortable and not get irritated or angry by anything around him. Therefore, he has two goals: to take a bath and maintain peace of mind (have no stress). He will fail the second one if he gets bothered by what is happening around him.

I know it might be hard to relate to going to a bathhouse because these can be rare to find, and you may have never even gone to one in your life (I know I haven't). However, you can apply this to pretty much any situation you face that you have experienced before. Before the next time you go to work (a stressful situation for most people), picture what you should expect when you get there. What do you know about your coworkers, and how should you expect them to act? What kind of boss do you have, and what interactions should you expect? Are there customers that you must interact with? What are some difficulties that you can have with them? Envision how your day goes and what should happen as it progresses. If you have been working at your job long enough, you should be able to answer these questions. If you expect the expected, you should have a better chance of keeping a level head if what you thought would happen happens. Remind yourself that your goal is not only to get through your day of work but also to keep your peace of mind as you do so.

I live in Southern California. Anyone who has driven the freeways in Southern California knows the plague of traffic that you will have to deal with. I used to get frustrated, irritated, annoyed, and angered when I was stuck in traffic trying to get somewhere (I don't think I am the only person who has felt this). However, now I aim to get where I want to go and keep my peace of mind. It is funny when you think about getting angry or irritated by sitting in traffic since it is not like you will get there any faster by feeling that way. You have two choices: stay calm or get angry; you will still get there at the same time, no matter your choice.

So, what do I do when I get ready to take the freeway these days?

I tell myself that I can expect it to take three times longer than it would if the traffic was not there. If you travel those freeways enough, you can predict which parts will be worse than others. I tell myself that I can expect a construction that never seems to end. Sometimes an accident causes a traffic jam, but it is often simply because too many cars are on the freeway. And when I get irritated, I take a moment, and a breath, then remind myself, should I have expected anything different? Relax, me being angry won't get me there any faster.

It does not have to apply just to situations in which you will interact with multiple people but can also be used in how you handle others on a one-on-one basis. Nobody is perfect, and everyone has their character flaws (including you). Some of those flaws might be easy for you to handle, and others might irritate or anger you.

Staying at a sober living with thirty men in varying stages of recovery is a test of skills of anger management and level-headedness. You are constantly witnessing arguments and complaints. I practice the principles of this chapter with my housemates by not being surprised or affected when they say or do things I know I should expect from them. Let's face it. I am living in a house with a bunch of addicts. And the more I get to know each of them personally, the more I understand the quirks of their personalities and what I should expect from them. Where I used to be the person who appeared unbothered because I bottled up my anger, now I am the person who is unbothered because I do not let things disturb me.

Think of a person who might frustrate you. Irritate you. Anger you. Is it a family member? Is it a friend? Is it someone you live with? What do they do that causes you to be frustrated, irritated, or angered? The next time you interact with them, whether on the phone or in person, remind yourself that these are the things you can expect that person to do or say and prepare yourself for them. Why get bent out of shape and disturbed when someone says or does something entirely in line with how they always are? It is crazy for you to expect them to be suddenly different.

> *"Say to yourself first thing in the morning: today I shall meet people who are meddling, ungrateful, aggressive, treacherous, malicious, unsocial."* – Marcus Aurelius, Meditations, 2.1.

In this passage from Marcus Aurelius, you can see how he tries to employ this tactic when he gets up in the morning and prepares for the day ahead. And look at the people he knew he would deal with. Remember that he was the emperor, which probably meant he had to interact with many personalities each day and was fully aware of people possibly trying to use him for their gain. So, he knew what to expect in the day ahead and prepared himself to interact with these people. It would allow him to approach these interactions level-headed rather than through the rash decisions of a person in power.

Anger, frustration, and irritability are emotions that our interactions with others can cause and are punishments we inflict upon ourselves. It is in our control to choose peace of mind and tranquility. Before any situation, ask yourself what you know about it and what you can expect. Then prepare yourself to...

Expect the expected.

"It's your own expectations that hurt you. Not the world you live in. Whatever happens in the world is real. What you think should happen is unreal. So people are hurt by their expectations. You know, you're not disappointed by the world, you are disappointed by your own projections." – Jacque Fresco

CHAPTER 5

Judge Events Correctly
(Wisdom)

Men are disturbed not by things, but by the views which they take of things. Thus death is nothing terrible, else it would have appeared so to Socrates. But the terror consists in our notion of death, that it is terrible.
– Chapter 5, Epictetus' Enchiridion.

———————

The concept discussed in this chapter is one of the most life-changing aspects of Stoicism. Many people who study this philosophy find that what Epictetus discusses here can radically impact their daily lives. And the first sentence of the chapter above is one of the most quoted lines you will come across when researching Stoicism. The core concept is changing how we view events and things that happen in our lives to reduce the negative emotions we feel solely due to how we perceive them.

All-or-Nothing thinking, also known as Black-and-White thinking, is common among people who suffer from addiction (Gaba 2019). It is a cognitive distortion or thinking error often treated through Cognitive Behavior Therapy in rehab or treatment with therapists. It is called All-or-Nothing thinking because the thinker views life as having only two options (all or nothing…black or white) with no possibilities in the middle or between. Addicts may develop this thinking because only having two options allows the brain to think less. But this becomes an issue for those who have dealt with addiction because our distorted thinking moves toward seeing things pessimistically, which is not a healthy state of mind. Having sobriety does not mean that this way of thinking will automatically end because our brains have gotten used to thinking of the world through this lens.

The Stoics saw that the two options that most of us use to judge things in life by (good or bad) have another option in the middle (indifference). This middle area can be challenging to achieve, as it will require us to suspend our judgment of events rather than putting a value (good or bad) on them. When we allow the choice of viewing things as bad, we open ourselves up to feeling negative emotions. Therefore, we need to learn how to shift our perspective towards judging things as being good or indifferent for mental stability. Since addicts move toward the negative perspective, this becomes another effective technique for recovery.

But how can we shift our perspective?

The choice is yours.

Good or bad is an opinion, and we control our opinions. As Epictetus points out at the beginning of this chapter, whenever we find ourselves bothered or disturbed by something that happens (judging it as something negative), it is not the event itself that concerns us but the view we decide to hold of it. A famous quote from William Shakespeare, who Stoicism influenced, gets at the heart of this concept wonderfully clearly.

"There is nothing either good or bad but thinking makes it so."
– William Shakespeare, Hamlet (Act 2, Scene 2).

Any event that happens in your life, whether it will be good or bad is all up to you; that is a choice you make. The event is simply just what it is. The judgment of how we will describe it is up to us, in our control.

To illustrate this, Epictetus discusses death. He picks this event because it is one that everyone will have to face in life, and at the same time, we commonly judge it as terrible and to be feared. However, death is merely something that happens. It is just death. Is it good? Is it bad? It is you who decides how you will view it.

He brings up the example of the philosopher Socrates to show that death should not be feared. Socrates did not die a natural death; he was given the death penalty for breaking the law of impiety (speaking against the gods) and corrupting the youth through his teachings. While he awaited his death, he had the opportunity to escape prison and flee the country. However, this would become a moral dilemma for him. He could escape prison and save his life, but everything he ever taught and stood for would be ruined. The meaning of his life that he had dedicated himself to would be gone and lost. Or he could accept his punishment and meet death, living the morals and values he tried to share with the world.

He chose death.

There is a reason the Stoics and philosophers throughout history have looked up to Socrates. He was a person who lived life by the virtue and excellence of character that he taught until the day that he died. He was an early example of living your philosophy of life.

When I first read this, I tried to understand how death could be considered anything other than bad. And then I remembered the death of my father. I was relieved when he died. I have always looked at it as a good thing. He had been battling cancer for years and reached the point where the doctors could do nothing other than send him home and wait for death. I remember being in the house during the last weeks, watching his condition deteriorate to where he was nearly comatose. So, when he finally passed away, I saw it as a good thing because he was free from the pain and wasting away.

"Dying should be one of the great events of life." – Alan Watts

As for fearing death, ask yourself, what is it you fear? We do not know what will happen to us when we die, and there is no reason to assume it will be horrible. If you think about it, death is the last event of the life that you have lived. Your grand finale. And what if that which comes after death is one of the most extraordinary things to ever happen to us? Nobody can say definitively that it is not. We spend our lives in fear of something inevitable while not truly understanding what comes after when we go through it. Death being something you must fear is a judgment you make on a subject you do not fully understand. You can erase the fear and change the judgment that you give to it.

When, therefore, we are hindered or disturbed, or grieved, let us never impute it to others, but to ourselves—that is, to our own views. It is the action of an uninstructed person to reproach others for his own misfortunes; of one entering upon instruction, to reproach himself; and one perfectly instructed, to reproach neither others nor himself. – Chapter 5, Epictetus' Enchiridion.

If you feel negative emotions over something that has happened to you, it is not the fault of the event itself or anyone else. The negative emotions you are feeling are a choice you make based on how you judge the event that occurred. And if you can view something as being negative, then you also have the choice to change that view to see it as something positive or, even better, completely neutral (indifferent).

This is important for those of us in recovery because sometimes when we see events as bad, we use them as an excuse to drink or use. At the same time, when we see something as good, we also use it as a reason to drink or use. Therefore, we should choose the middle and see events simply for what they are with no value judgment placed on them (indifferent).

When I went through my last alcoholic bottom, I was homeless and jobless. The clothes I wore were my only possession, and I had only a few dollars left in the bank. When I first looked back at this event, I judged it as being something horrible. I could not believe that my life had gotten to that point, and I could never imagine ever being in a situation like that. It filled me with feelings of regret and shame, and in a state of deep depression. As I gained my sobriety, I looked at this event in a positive light, seeing that it was only through experiencing that moment that I finally realized my addiction and the motivation to do something about it. I viewed the same event in different ways. In one way, I judged it as bad, and it filled me with negative emotions. On the other, I see it as good, and the negative feelings disappear.

But how do I see it now?

There was a time in my life when I only had the clothes I was wearing and a few dollars in the bank. That is all that it is. It wasn't a bad thing because it led to my recovery. It wasn't good because I had self-destructed my life and hurt many people who cared for me. It was just something that happened to me. Now it lies in the past, out of my control, and is not a part of my present. Therefore, these days I am indifferent to it.

Regarding the concepts of good or bad, Stoics believe we can find only these two things within ourselves. Good is when you are practicing the four virtues of Stoicism in your life. Bad is the vices representing the opposite of those virtues (uncourageous, lacking self-control, injustice, irrational, etc.). Therefore, good or bad can only exist through you and the actions that you commit.

However, for things outside our control, we have to learn to judge them as being indifferent and accept them just as they are placing no value judgment upon them. Since other people are outside of your control, this will mean that what they do cannot be seen as good or bad but will have to be looked at as indifferent. And as stated above, the past is out of your control; even though it is your past, look at it from the view of indifference since there is nothing you can do to change it (trust me, this is one of the most freeing aspects of Stoicism for an addict). These significant concepts introduced here will be returned to throughout this book to allow you to gain a deeper understanding of them and how to apply them to your life practically.

Epictetus ends this chapter by saying that an uninstructed person who has learned nothing of what is being taught in this book will blame the "bad" things that happen in life on another person…God…or whoever they can point their finger at. A person learning will only blame themselves because Stoicism teaches no person can harm you unless you let them do so. But the enlightened person has learned what is instructed here, that there should be no judgments about anything that happens and that what happens is simply all that it is. They will not blame others or themselves because they see events as truly what they are and place no value judgments on them. You cannot be harmed if you see nothing as being bad. To use another term we learn in recovery, the enlightened person lives by the ideal of "it is what it is."

Neither good…

Nor bad…

It just is.

"Everything is as good or bad as our opinion makes it." – C.S. Lewis, Till We Have Faces: A Myth Retold.

CHAPTER 6

The Slippery Slope of Pride
(Wisdom)

Be not elated at any excellence not your own. If a horse should be elated, and say, "I am handsome," it might be endurable. But when you are elated and say, "I have a handsome horse," know that you are elated only on the merit of the horse. What then is your own? The use of the phenomena of existence. So that when you are in harmony with nature in this respect, you will be elated with some reason; for you will be elated at some good of your own. – Chapter 6, Epictetus' Enchiridion.

B e proud of your sobriety. There is nothing wrong with that. We can proudly take the chips and celebrate the anniversaries of our sobriety date because it represents something about who we are. It is an excellence of character that we have chosen and are living. Or, as Epictetus says above, it is a good of our own.

It belongs to us.

But is pride good or bad? We often think that pride can be a bad thing because it is the opposite of being humble, and if you like to follow the seven deadly sins, you know it is one of them. However, pride can be something that can make us feel good as a person when we have accomplished something and have positive emotions associated with it. Like the discussion of desire and aversion, whether we are using pride correctly will depend on what we are being proud of. And hopefully, by the end of this chapter, you might understand why it may not even be helpful or needed in your own life.

Epictetus uses the example of a horse in this chapter to examine how we abuse pride. He jokes that if a horse could say that it is handsome, that would be fine, but if you are proud of having a handsome horse, does that belong to you? Even if you own the horse, its characteristics belong to it and not to you.

To modernize this example, consider cars and how some proudly show them off. They will tell you about every detail their car has and its capabilities. But you are not a car, and you are not your car. Any characteristics of the car that you own belong to the vehicle and not to you. And the worst part is that at least a horse, being a living creature, is probably genetically one of a kind, while your car has most likely been produced many times and owned by other people.

> "You are not your job. You are not how much money you have in the bank. You are not the car that you drive. You are not the contents of your wallet...." – From the movie Fight Club.

One thing I love about Fight Club (both the book and movie) is its existential and philosophical debate on the meaning of life and what is truly valuable. It is the same issue the Stoics attempted to solve but came up with a different answer. But in the quote from the movie above (the book has a similar one, but the film one is more drawn out), you can see a discussion of the things that people will often find pride in while pointing out that it is not who you are. Your job is what you do. Other people probably have the same or similar positions; would that mean they are the same as you? Your money is an external possession, and so is any credit card inside your wallet. Other people have just as much money as you or the same credit card; does this mean that you are similar?

None of these things say anything about the person that you are.

Some people might think that all the things mentioned above (job, car, money, etc.) could be something you are proud of due to your accomplishments in life. The problem with finding self-worth in all these external things is that they are temporary, and then you can become addicted to achieving more and more to keep the feeling going (Amodeo 2015). In our recovery, we need to break the cycle of addiction, even if that addiction is achievement. And as discussed in previous chapters, all these things are external to us and can be lost at any moment. Having pride and self-worth in things such as these set you up for negative emotions if you lose them. Because how can you see yourself the same way if the stuff you base your value on is gone?

This is the slippery slope of pride.

To begin this chapter, I discussed the pride that we can have in our own recovery. But this could pose a danger as well. What happens if we relapse? We can already struggle with self-worth amid addiction, so if sobriety becomes our pride, it could be even harder to pull out of relapse when we have destroyed what we placed so much value on. I have had too many conversations with people in recovery kicking themselves for losing the sober time they once had, watching them plagued with negative emotions with a mind stuck on the lost pride of the past.

Beyond the impact of our self-worth when losing what we pride ourselves in, there are other issues. Psychiatrists and therapists have discovered certain character flaws within an individual that are signaled through the display of pride. One of these discovered flaws is that people who often show pride have an inflated view of themselves and little care for others (Amodeo 2015). Showing off the things you are proud of can sometimes make people feel like they are less than you and possibly illicit feelings of shame for not having what you have. This is the exact opposite of Stoic justice, in which the things we do should take others into consideration.

Another fascinating flaw is that people who frequently show too much pride actually have low self-worth and feelings of shame that they are trying to hide. Therefore, pride is a mask trying to hide flaws within an individual's character. It is a symptom of something wrong rather than a display of something right. Stoics would say that the value you have in life is tied to the person you are…your character. So, with the goals we reach and the things we achieve, feel good about them but focus more on what they say about your character (hard-working, persistent, resilient, etc.). Do not place all the weight on the achievement itself because what happens if it disappears (lose the job, the car, your sobriety, etc.)? The achievement of goals can sometimes be temporary, as they can be lost because of things outside of your control, but who you are can never be taken away by someone else.

In the eyes of the Stoics, there is no reason to display outward pride by showcasing our achievements to others. They remind us that the opinions held by others lie beyond our control and should be treated with indifference. The only opinion that holds true significance is the one we have of ourselves. If our need to show off our accomplishments leads others to feel inferior, it indicates a failure in practicing Stoic justice—valuing the well-being of all.

The slippery slope of pride rests in the idea that, often, we are proud of the wrong things in life. And if we feel the need to show off pride, it could be the symptom of underlying flaws we try to hide. If we are going to be proud of anything, it must focus on the excellence of our character. However, in general, the more we can avoid pride and focus on being happy for who we are, the better off we will be.

"...pride, that invisible bone that keeps a neck stiff." – Stephen King, The Gunslinger.

CHAPTER 7

Be Prepared for Death's Voyage
(Courage, Wisdom)

As in a voyage, when the ship is at anchor, if you go on shore to get water, you may amuse yourself with picking up a shellfish or a truffle in your way, but your thoughts ought to be bent toward the ship, and perpetually attentive, lest the captain should call, and then you must leave all these things, that you may not have to be carried on board the vessel, bound like a sheep; thus likewise in life, if, instead of a truffle or shellfish, such a thing as a wife or a child be granted you, there is no objection; but if the captain calls, run to the ship, leave all these things, and never look behind. But if you are old, never go far from the ship, lest you should be missing when called for. – Chapter 7, Epictetus' Enchiridion.

———————

Death is our ultimate voyage. It is the one that awaits all of us, no matter what our station in life is. It is the one voyage we must embark immediately on when we are called to take it. And as discussed throughout this book, we must learn to accept our mortality.

In this chapter, Epictetus is talking about life and death. More specifically, the preparation for death; our great and final voyage. He compares our lives as if we are going on shore while the ship that will be our death is at anchor with a captain that will call for us when it is our time to die. He discusses life in simple terms. While on shore, we get food and nutrients for our body (water), do things to amuse ourselves, and even pick up various possessions throughout life (shellfish and truffle). We may even be lucky enough to get married or have a lifelong partner. We may even be more blessed with being able to have children. However, the main thing to notice with this life on shore is that we are getting external items outside our control as we live.

There is this famous saying, "You can't take it with you." The basic idea is the same premise of this chapter; when we are called to that last voyage, we must be ready to leave all the things we have gained. And even if we do not want to leave this life ashore when the call comes, we will still be carried away against our will (bound like sheep).

Accepting death remains a profound challenge for humanity, which is precisely why the Stoics dedicated considerable discussion to this topic. They recognized it as a fundamental flaw in the human psyche. Ironically, the one inevitable event that every individual will confront is the very one they often avoid contemplating. When thoughts of mortality do arise, many people seek ways to evade it, trying to conceive methods to circumvent the inevitable. Even a whole industry called cryonics profits off this desire not to leave life behind and attempt to refuse the call to the voyage. At the cost of $200,000, you can have your body frozen when death calls or spend $80,000 to have just your DNA frozen, with the idea that someday they might revive and heal you (Guzman, 2016). However, the government notes that the person is dead, so the companies have no obligation to attempt to revive their customers. In other words, people are spending money to fight against the voyage, even though the ship has already sailed. What great things could they have done with this money rather than waste it on the inevitable?

"And if God is pleased to add another day, we should welcome it with glad hearts. That man is happiest, and is secure in his own possession of himself, who can await the morrow without apprehension. When a man has said: "I have lived!" every morning he arises he receives a bonus." – Seneca, On Old Age.

Fighting against and not accepting our final voyage of death can lead to us wasting the precious resources we have. As with cryonics, it could be a waste of money. But more importantly, it can be a waste of our most precious resource...time. The assumption that we have countless days ahead of us can lead someone to think there is always more time to do the things they want to do in life. In essence, we waste time ashore and fight the last call because we have spent our lives not getting ready for it.

We must spend our time preparing for our eventual death since we do not know the moment it will come. Each day we wake to face is a bonus day we have been blessed with. Do not become too attached to your possessions since you can't take them with you. Spend every day with your loved ones as if it were your last, making the most of each moment you are around them. You need to live your life each day, telling yourself that you have lived the life you desired. And that you are ready if you are not given another day on this earth.

I know that sometimes for those of us in recovery, we can look back at all the time we wasted on our addictions. We get lost in thoughts of the days we have thrown away and all the things we could have done. But the time is now to live. So let go of the past and focus on the present. And each new day in which we get to live is a bonus.

When the captain calls us on that final voyage, we must leave everything behind and not look back. And if we have lived the best life we could while ashore, then we have no reason to resist the final voyage.

"To die will be an awfully big adventure." – *J.M. Barrie, Peter Pan.*

CHAPTER 8

Wish for All That Happens
(Courage, Wisdom)

Demand not that events should happen as you wish; but wish them to happen as they do happen, and you will go on well. – Chapter 8, Epictetus' Enchiridion.

———

Thy will be done.

Let go and let God.

Accept life on life's terms.

The idea that we must learn to accept that everything cannot go the way we want is something that you commonly hear in rehab programs and the rooms of Alcoholics Anonymous or any of its variations.

As we lose control over our addictions, we can often shift our sphere of control to other parts of our lives to feel that we have at least some grip on life (Milios 2019). So, we try to control situations beyond us, such as relationships (partners, family, friends, etc.), work, rules we should follow (breaking laws is common), and many other daily interactions. Since we do not have control over our addiction, we want to control and have the world work the way we want it.

When we enter recovery, we accept that this kind of control that we tried to exert on the world is something we can no longer do. After all, if we genuinely look at the destruction our attempts to control everything had on our relationships and positions in life, it can be quite apparent why we cannot be this way in sobriety. Besides, by this point in the book, you should realize that what we attempted to control were things we never honestly had control over. Therefore, if we are going to be successful in our recovery, we must change the old ways of our addiction, release that outer sphere of control, and begin to accept life on life's terms.

Stoics, however, bring this to an even higher level. Rather than just accepting what happens in life as it comes at you, why not wish for everything that happens to you? Because if we can see that all things that happen to us are as we wish, then we will never have to deal with anything in life that is not going the way we want it to go. This is a Stoic concept now referred to as *amor fati* (love of fate). It is this idea of joyfully accepting what happens in life, even if it contains moments that some people would judge as bad or catastrophic (Robertson 2018, 91). Now, this will not be an issue during the good times. It is easy to wish for what comes at you if everything is going your way. But how do you wish for the tough parts of life?

"If you work hard to do what is right, do not be upset by roadblocks; think about how many things in your life haven't turned out as you wanted them to, but as they should have."
– Musonius Rufus

Think of some of the toughest challenges that you have faced in life. What did you learn from them? How did they strengthen you? How was your character changed for the better by surviving through them? The Stoics realized great things could come from the difficulties we face, so there should be no reason to look upon them in a negative mind state.

I think people who have survived addiction and chosen a path of recovery know this concept all too well. Recovery can be very difficult. It is much easier to just stay within our addictions. And to take on the challenge of recovery is very much a character-building process. It takes courage, strength, and resilience to successfully overcome addiction. We do not just become sober when we choose recovery; we change as a person and develop our character in healthier ways.

Throughout his book, *The Stoic Challenge*, William Irvine discusses how a person can use this perspective to wish for even the most challenging parts of life. He learned through his journey in Stoicism that when he faced a difficult situation, it gave him a chance to practice what he was learning. When life is going well, it is easy to make the right decisions and be good. However, when a person faces difficulties, you get a genuine test of your character. Can you still be virtuous, seeking character excellence when things are not going your way? With time, William Irvine discovered that viewing difficulties as opportunities to apply his learning led to increased calmness and resilience in the face of life's challenges. Gradually, he found himself eagerly anticipating further opportunities to test and refine his character. Embracing the Stoic mindset allowed him to approach life's obstacles with a newfound sense of confidence and readiness.

This becomes another Stoic strategy known to modern psychology as *the framing effect*, in which how we characterize a situation can profoundly affect how we emotionally respond to it

(Irvine 2019, 17). Suppose we can frame the problematic situations in our lives as opportunities to test our character. In that case, we have a better chance of having a positive emotional response to them rather than a negative one. As Epictetus stated in this chapter, we are better off if we wish everything to happen exactly as they do. Good or bad (even though we should not put judgments on things)...easy or difficult...all things in life that happen to us can serve a purpose. Learn to love the fate that life brings to you each day in which you exist.

How would you feel if you got what you wished for every day?

"You cannot control what happens to you, but you can control your attitude toward what happens to you, and in that, you will be mastering change rather than allowing it to master you." – Brian Tracy

CHAPTER 9

There Is No Excuse
(Courage, Wisdom)

Sickness is an impediment to the body, but not to the will unless itself pleases. Lameness is an impediment to the leg, but not to the will; and say this to yourself with regard to everything that happens. For you will find it to be an impediment to something else, but not truly to yourself.
– Chapter 9, Epictetus' Enchiridion.

———

One thing that addicts are quite good at is creating excuses for their choices. In the depths of my addictions, I had plenty of reasons for needing to drink or use when good things happened. I definitely could provide even more excuses for why I needed to drink or use when bad things happened. Of course, there were plenty of reasons why I did not have to go to rehab or get any help for my addictions. And I did not want to hear what anyone else had to say because I am so different from everyone else, and nobody could understand what I was going through (the ultimate excuse many of us addicts use).

I think that this is one of the most powerful parts of the Alcoholics Anonymous approach, which relies significantly on empathy and shared experiences. Instead of addressing individuals as mere addicts, the program encourages sharing personal stories. By narrating their own experiences, individuals discover similarities with others, debunking the illusion of being isolated and different from everyone else. This empathetic connection undermines the notion that they are alone in their struggles and helps break down barriers that addiction can create.

When we made excuses for why we had to use, we were rationalizing our behaviors—giving reasons it was okay for us to choose our addictions or any actions (lying, cheating, stealing, etc.) to allow us to keep them going. And it is not like sobriety will suddenly cause this thinking pattern to disappear. It is what we have grown used to. Yes, you may no longer choose to partake in your drug of choice, but do you still make excuses for other destructive behaviors and actions that you commit?

To the Stoics, the rational mind is the greatest asset that any person has. We are given this unique ability to logically think about situations that we are in and choose the right course of action. If you believe in God, then you would view this as one of the greatest gifts God has given to you. However, suppose science is more your belief. In that case, many scientists consider our ability to reason one of the key characteristics evolution has worked on in humans, allowing us to thrive on this planet despite our physical limitations compared to other species. This chapter points out that nothing stands in your way of using your rational mind to make the right choices (living a life of virtue).

Epictetus focuses this chapter on sickness and bodily injury, which, if you recall, are things that reside out of the realm of our control. He had to live with a crippled leg throughout his life, possibly from an injury by an enslaver when he was young. Seneca struggled with illness and was close to death in his younger years. James Stockdale was tortured throughout his time as a prisoner of war. None of these men used the excuse of their injuries or health as a reason not to live the principles of Stoicism. These were all things that happened to their bodies but could not harm the rational mind and their ability to choose correctly.

If an obstacle impedes your life, remind yourself of what that obstacle affects, and at the same time, tell yourself that it does not stop you from having the ability of your choice and the person you want to be. For example, if you're sick, it is an obstacle for your body, but you still have a working, rational mind to make the right choices. If, like Epictetus, your leg is injured, remind yourself that it only affects your leg. Remember from the chapter on pride that you are not your job, car, bank account, or what's in your wallet. Anything that affects these aspects of your life does not affect who you are. Therefore, for anything that occurs in life, take a moment, tell yourself what it truly affects, and then notice that you still have power over your mind and the person you choose to be.

For those of us in recovery, we already live the essence of this chapter in a way. We acknowledge we suffer from a sickness or disease by the name of addiction but choose not to allow it to get in the way of living sobriety. No matter what happens to us in life, we do not have the option to turn back toward our addictions as a way in which to deal with them. There is no good excuse to give us a reason to return to our drug of choice.

But what about people still lost in addiction?

I know it may seem like an impossible task to grab hold of the rational mind and make the right choice. The addiction itself seems as if it is holding a knife to the neck of our rational thought, threatening to kill if we decide to quit.

But this threat is an empty one.

The first step that everyone who has ever recovered from any form of addiction has been one in which the rational mind is harnessed. Merely the thought of saying I have a problem and I am going to do something about it is a rational decision. In that sprouting moment of recovery, we say that even though we may suffer from addiction, we will listen to the logical side of our mind screaming at us and make a change. In essence, it is only through the power of the rational mind that we can be released from the deathly grips of our drug of choice.

The Stoics would say, now use this same rational mind and thinking that powers you through your recovery in all aspects of life. When something happens, remind yourself of what is affecting you. Use the techniques of Stoicism to understand what you have in your control and let go of what is out of it. Remember to alter your perspective of the events (how you judge things and the Stoic challenge). And realize that none of these things affects your rational mind and your ability to choose the right course of action.

Choose who you want to be as a person and live it.

The only one standing in your way is yourself.

"My body could stand the crutches but my mind couldn't stand the sideline." – Michael Jordan

CHAPTER 10

Strength Through Adversity
(Courage, Temperance, Wisdom)

Upon every accident, remember to turn toward yourself and inquire what faculty you have for its use. If you encounter a handsome person, you will find continence the faculty needed; if pain, then fortitude; if reviling, then patience. And when thus habituated, the phenomena of existence will not overwhelm you. – Chapter 10, Epictetus' Enchiridion.

E arlier in the book, I had discussed how William Irvine described in his work *The Stoic Challenge* how he learned to take the difficulties in his life and turn them into something positive that he could end up wishing for. In this chapter, Epictetus delves into the foundations of this challenge.

> *"Calamity is the occasion of virtue, and a spur to a great mind...Nay, many times a calamity turns to our advantage; and great ruins have but made way to greater glories."– Seneca, Of a Happy Life, Chapter VIII.*

DEREK CASTLEMAN & EPICTETUS

The Stoics realized that the way of life they were proposing to live differed vastly from most of the world, addict or non-addict. And because of this, it was not something you would learn how to do overnight perfectly. It would take practice and training. It is a progress over perfection form of thinking. In fact, throughout many of their writings, you will find them comparing living Stoicism as if you were an athlete in training. Each day we have opportunities to practice the principles of the philosophy in a way that we can continually strengthen our character.

In this chapter, you can see how Epictetus is giving insight into how we can approach challenging situations we face in life and see them as opportunities to grow from them. Whenever you face an accident...hardship...challenge, you need to ask yourself what you have inside you to meet this situation and grow stronger. Maybe even try to look at the situation and tell yourself what you will train and gain in character by overcoming it.

The first challenge he discusses is what you can gain from a situation where you encounter an attractive (handsome) person. The Stoics were not anti-sex at all; they just promoted a view that we must have healthy sexual relations, which can be critical for those who have dealt with addiction. Not only do people suffer from sexual addiction, but many addicts have shown issues with sexual behavior.

Sex and drugs both affect the brain's reward center, so many addicts engage in promiscuous sexual behavior when under the influence since they feed off each other to create a more intense experience (Bradford Health Services n.d.). One of the main reasons it is suggested to avoid sexual relationships for at least the first year of sobriety is the connection between sex and using. Numerous stories of relapse exist in which individuals in recovery took part in unhealthy sexual relations that pushed them on a direct path back to their addiction. Therefore, Epictetus points out that being able to overcome the feelings of sexual desire when you see an attractive person is a way in which you can train and strengthen your ability of self-restraint (continence).

It is an opportunity for growth.

Are you in pain?

See this as an opportunity to develop the virtue of courage as you push through it and not let it affect your burgeoning character.

Did someone insult you or say something you did not like?

See this as a chance to develop patience.

Many of us in recovery need to practice anger management, and Stoics felt it was something that many people, in general, struggled with, which is why this subject will be returned to in later chapters.

Stoics view we need to gain control over the passions that we encounter in life. Now, I know it can seem like advocating for a life without passion is one that no person would want to live. But you need to understand that passions to the Stoics are irrational, excessive, unnatural (unhealthy) forms of fear and desire that are the consequence of feelings of pain and pleasure (Robertson 2018, 21). As you can see, they are those unhealthy and excessive feelings that can cause us to make irrational decisions. Since Stoicism advocates strengthening the rational mind, these forms of passion would weaken it.

It should be clear why they have this view based on what I discussed in this chapter. If strong sexual desire causes someone to make the irrational decision of relapsing, then that person needs to overcome those feelings to make the right choices. And how many irrational actions have you committed when you were in the grips of anger, actions that you would regret once you calmed down?

Therefore, you need to train yourself in patience so you will not be carried away with anger.

"Difficulties strengthen the mind, as labor does the body."
– Seneca

The Stoic challenge is strength training for your mind in the same manner that working out strengthens the body. It is about learning self-control and discipline when facing the passions that can cause us to lose our rational minds. Every day, everyone comes across moments where they can learn more about themselves and grow in character. Make a habit of responding to the challenges you face by taking a breath and then asking yourself what you can gain from this situation and what abilities you will work out through it. The more you do this, the stronger you will get, and the less likely your passions or emotions will carry you away when you meet adversity.

"Everything negative - pressure, challenges - is all an opportunity for me to rise."– Kobe Bryant

CHAPTER 11

We Borrow That Which We Possess
(Courage, Justice, Temperance, Wisdom)

Never say of anything, "I have lost it," but, "I have restored it." Has your child died? It is restored. Has your wife died? She is restored. Has your estate been taken away? That likewise is restored. "But it was a bad man who took it." What is it to you by whose hands he who gave it has demanded it again? While he permits you to possess it, hold it as something not your own, as do travelers at an inn. – Chapter 10, Epictetus' Enchiridion.

Delving further into how to deal with the loss of possessions and loved ones, Epictetus provides another perspective on how we should look at the situation, bringing together several of the concepts he has discussed up to this point.

The easiest way to understand this chapter is to start with the last sentence. We must think of life as travelers staying at a hotel. Because what do we do when we stay at one? We have a bed to use (hopefully one better than at home). We have a shower and a toilet. Closets and dressers for our clothes. Lights. Internet. Cable television. Maybe a

DEREK CASTLEMAN & EPICTETUS

pool and jacuzzi on site. Perhaps a suite with a living room and a kitchen. And maybe, if we are fortunate, a jacuzzi tub is inside the room. We stay there for those days and nights; we can use all these things as if they were our own. And I do not know about you, but I appreciate them as if they are my own. However, when the check-out time comes, we return the room to the owner who allowed it to be used, and it is now no longer in our possession.

We must think of what we possess in life like staying in a hotel room. They exist in that realm of external things we do not control, which means they can be taken away from us at any moment. When these possessions remain in our life, we are simply borrowing them, and the world, whether it be other people, God, or nature itself, can take them back from us. Epictetus suggests we need to change our perspective and consider all things we possess as not being lost to us but returned (restored). He suggests this mainly because we usually have no issue with returning things to their owner, but we do struggle with the feeling of losing something that we viewed as our own. It is another strategy to alter your way of thinking to help lessen the occurrence of negative emotions.

People will often say that they have lost their job. But was the job actually lost? Most likely, they were laid off or fired, and they returned the job to the employer to hire someone else or eliminate it. The concept of at-will employment found in most states in the United States literally says that an employer can terminate a position anytime without explanation. The job can be returned to the employer whenever they feel like it (although some rules apply).

Was the car lost or repossessed and returned to the lender who originally paid for the vehicle? Was the apartment lost or an eviction or nonrenewal of the lease that returned it to the owner? And sometimes, the house was not lost; it was foreclosed on and returned to the lender. You can even apply this to relationships. The partner you have in life allows you to be with them, and they can take it back any moment they want to so that they can give the opportunity to another person.

A harsh reality for those of us in recovery is that we may have lost (returned) these things because of our own behaviors while amid our addictions. Multiple times during my cycles of recovery and relapses, I would find myself "returning" all that I had as I would end up homeless, jobless, carless, and with no possessions. Sometimes we may even resent the people who had taken them from us. So many recovery programs want you to look back at what you did and what you lost during your addictions because they want you to see the role you played, which caused the borrower to take back what they lent you.

The things we have in life come from outside sources. They are external to us. Which means they can be taken away. And if another person gave them to us, since we have no control over the actions of others, we have no control over whether or not we will lose them. Even as Epictetus points out, if the person who takes it away from us is bad or we think it is wrong, they take it. They gave it to us, so they have the power to take it back. So, one of the harsh realities of accepting the things that happen outside your control is simply that...you must accept them...you have no choice.

But what if it was not a person?

"The Lord giveth, and the Lord taketh away." – The Bible, Job, 1:21.

All material things that we own come from the earth. Even if manufacturers built them, the resources used come from the planet itself. Whether your beliefs lie in the realm of God or nature itself, you could see this idea of returning even further. For example, natural disasters are often called Acts of God, and these events can quickly return everything we own back to the world it came out of. And even beyond natural disasters, when things we own break or no longer have a purpose, we send them to the garbage dump, where they are literally returned to the earth from which their materials have come out.

Epictetus returns to the concept of the death of a loved one since this is the most brutal loss most will have to deal with. If you believe in God, you can view all of life as a gift from God. However, it is also in God's hands to choose when life ends. There is a Christian view in which God calls us home in death, and this concept perfectly aligns with the idea that we are not lost but returned. And if you do not believe in God, then you should think of it as if we are born from the world, and our bodies are built from the materials we take in from the environment. When we die, we simply return the materials we had incorporated from the planet within our bodies for reuse for other purposes, possibly even into other living organisms.

We need to treat the things in life like when we stay in a hotel. We enjoy them. Appreciate them. Make the most of our time with them. However, we do this with the understanding of impermanence and that when we are asked to give them back, we have no choice but to return them. Unlike a hotel, the moment they may ask us to return them has an unknown check-out date. Therefore, always appreciate them while they are in your possession, but be prepared to return them.

"Nothing is lost, nothing is created, everything is transformed." – *Antoine de Lavoisier*

CHAPTER 12

Practicing Indifference for Peace of Mind
(Courage, Justice, Temperance, Wisdom)

If you would improve, lay aside such reasonings as these: "If I neglect my affairs, I shall not have a maintenance; if I do not punish my servant, he will be good for nothing." For it were better to die of hunger, exempt from grief and fear, than to live in affluence with perturbation; and it is better that your servant should be bad than you unhappy. – Chapter 12, Epictetus' Enchiridion.

B y this point in the book, Epictetus advises us to abandon certain reasonings that lead to unnecessary distress. Throughout the book, Epictetus skillfully weaves bigger-picture arguments and logical explanations behind Stoic thought, connecting them to practical applications in daily life.

In this chapter, he returns to the concept of All-or-Nothing thinking that was discussed earlier in the book. Remember, this is the tendency (especially among addicts) to see the world from the view of only two extremes: usually positive or negative things. And the issue with addicts is that we generally push our perception of events and ourselves toward the negative side. I concluded that chapter by discussing how Stoics advocate we need to see the things that occur outside of ourselves, not at extremes but this middle ground of indifference. In this chapter, Epictetus discusses how we can practice indifference and why it is significant for a healthy mental state.

He begins by giving examples of some All-or-Nothing thinking by presenting:

1. Someone who is neglecting their affairs.
2. Someone who is having issues with a servant (remember, he lived in a time of enslaved people as he once was one).

I will modernize these examples to make it easier to see what he is discussing. We can think of the person neglecting their affair as someone similar to a workaholic or obsessed with making money. They feel this need to focus so much of their life solely on pursuing money, fearing that they may not have enough to provide for themselves the lifestyle they think they must have. If they do not obsessively make money, they cannot survive.

Many of us may not have had a servant tend to our daily needs, but we probably have all dealt with servers when dining out. And if you have gone to enough restaurants, you may have dealt with orders being wrong, food taking a long time to be made, an inattentive server, or simply lousy service in general. The individual in Epictetus's example would need to punish the worker (leave no tip, report to the manager, etc.) for correcting the behavior. If they do not do something in response to what they felt was inadequate service, the worker will continue to act this way (be good for nothing or worthless).

You can see the All-or-Nothing thinking in these examples. If I do not do this (obsess over making money or punish a worker), then this horrible thing (I won't be able to support my lifestyle, or the worker will be worthless) will happen.

Epictetus follows this up with why we must get over this All-or-Nothing thinking. The first is a bit of an extreme example in saying that it is better to die with hunger without grief or fear rather than to live a wealthy life that is constantly anxious. However, the point he is making is that it is better for a person to deal with something that happens to their body (hunger) than the self-inflicted anguish of fear and anxiety of the mind. James Stockdale had noted during his time as a prisoner that it was not the pain that was inflicted on the body that brought a man down, but what truly broke him was the feeling of shame (Stockdale 1993, 19). The captors were torturing their prisoners because they wanted to break into their minds. After all, that is when they had truly destroyed the person and had control over them.

Some of us in recovery may have lost so much in the depths of our addictions (careers, relationships, money, possessions) that we can feel that we need to regain those things in our lives. Will having all those things back give you a better life? Did having all those things in life make you mentally stable before? We who have lost all that we had through addiction can have a unique insight into this chapter. What we lost were not the most valuable things in life because we still found that it was not enough and something was missing, so we tried to fill that void with our addictions.

Recent studies have shown that younger and wealthier individuals have higher levels of anxiety and depression (almost twice as much) than less wealthy people of the same age (Browne 2013). And they find higher anxiety levels in more affluent countries than poorer ones (Sheridan 2017). Many people think money buys happiness but often find that once they achieve it, money brings additional problems and stresses. It could be stress from higher demanding jobs or anxiety because of fears that they may not have enough money and possibly lose it (Lutz 2017). As Epictetus says, it would be better to go hungry than deal with constant fear, anxiety, and depression over concerns about money.

With someone serving you, the Stoics would have two different ways to view the scenario. First, remember that we need to not put judgments on the things that others do. Good and bad only exist within us. Besides, we do not know why the person acted that way. For all you know, at that moment, they might struggle with personal issues (loss of a loved one, the ending of a relationship, etc.). Things could also have affected the restaurant that night, like being short-staffed. The interactions we will have with most of the people we come across in our lives will be a mere blip in the totality of their existence, which shrouds from our vision the accurate knowledge of why they may behave in the way they are.

Beyond the virtue of justice and consideration of others (the server), the Stoics would also want you to focus on what could happen if you let the interactions disrupt your emotions. Why waste your meal or the company you are with by being in a bad mood? It would be best to find gratitude in the food you are eating and the people you are with. Have you ever allowed someone else's behavior to impact your emotions, ruining the moment in which you were living? How did that go for you?

You can apply this same thinking when dealing with any worker serving or helping you. If you have people you manage or supervise at work. When you go to any store...theme park...the movies... sporting events...mass transit...etc. When you are on the phone with someone who works in customer service. There is never a good reason why you should lose your mind and ruin your emotional state due to the performance of someone offering you some kind of service.

It is best to maintain your peace of mind.

Before I go to the next part of the chapter, I want to return to the concept of preferred indifference. The Stoics are not telling a person to live without money, relationships, a place to live, and possessions. Of course, it is nice to have these things. However, they say these things are unnecessary for a happy life. If they were, anyone with these things would automatically be happy, but we know that is false. Stoics believe anyone can achieve happiness by simply being a good person (living that life of virtue). Happiness does not require possessions; it simply just requires a good you. They call these other aspects of life preferred indifferents because they are unnecessary, and since they are outside our control, they lie between good and bad. Stoics call them preferred because, of course, it would be nice to have them. They are like icing on the cake of life, but they should still be preferred and not needed. We set ourselves up for mental trouble when we turn them into needs.

Begin therefore with little things. Is a little oil spilled or a little wine stolen? Say to yourself, "This is the price paid for peace and tranquility; and nothing is to be had for nothing." And when you call your servant, consider that it is possible he may not come at your call; or, if he does, that he may not do what you wish. But it is not at all desirable for him, and very undesirable for you, that it should be in his power to cause you any disturbance. – Chapter 12, Epictetus' Enchiridion.

Epictetus finishes this chapter by advising on how to respond to events with that middle-ground view of indifference. He suggests starting with the little things. You spill over some food… it's just a bit of food lost. Some place you wanted to go to today is closed…you can find another place or return tomorrow. You got a stain on your new piece of clothing that you bought… it's just clothing. You missed the bus…another one will be coming. Someone is driving too slow in front of you…you can pass them up if possible or continue to drive behind them.

A widely known saying is, "don't sweat the small stuff." That is basically what he is presenting here. Why get all worked up over these minor inconveniences in life? Isn't it better to have peace and tranquility? This is the essence of indifference. Do not get mentally disturbed when things do not work as you want; take them for what they are and move on. These are mere trifles in the grand scheme of life and all of the universe. Besides, getting your mind out of balance due to things will not change the fact they have happened.

Practicing indifference is quite challenging to do. I know I found it to be that way with me at first. But follow Epictetus's advice from above. You start with the little things and begin working your way up to bigger ones. While writing this book, I have dealt with countless job rejections as I attempt to change careers, a $10,000 tax debt placed on me to pay because I was wronged by someone else, and I am still at my sober living after three years of being unable to move out with my girlfriend of seven years since I do not have the money. I could judge all these things as being bad. Get depressed or angry about the situations that I am dealing with. But would that change them in any way whatsoever? No. These situations would still exist regardless of my mental and emotional state. Therefore, I just look at them with indifference so I can live each day with tranquility while keeping control of my mind to find ways to approach and solve each of these challenges.

When dealing with people who might destroy your tranquility, Epictetus suggests that whoever it is can do what they are going to do, but do not give them the power to disturb you. When someone makes you angry or anxious, you are literally handing them the power over your mind and allowing them to do that to you. Using the example of the restaurant, if you let the service make you unhappy, then you have given that person power over your mind to ruin your present moment. You have given them control of your emotions. Therefore, if you find that someone is bringing up negative feelings in your life, you need to take a moment and a breath and tell yourself that you will not let this person have the power. They can do whatever they are going to do that you may disapprove of, but the one thing they cannot do is disturb your mind. You have power over your mind, and it is your choice to whom you give that control.

Keep it in your grip.

Hold on to your power.

"Start the daily practice of not letting the little things bother you! If the little things ruin you, what's going to happen when the big things come along? Start practicing now for your big challenges in life." – Bryant McGill

Courage to Be Different
(Courage)

If you would improve, be content to be thought foolish and dull with regard to externals. Do not desire to be thought to know anything; and though you should appear to others to be somebody, distrust yourself. For be assured, it is not easy at once to keep your will in harmony with nature and to secure externals; but while you are absorbed in the one, you must of necessity neglect the other. – Chapter 13, Epictetus' Enchiridion.

The Stoics knew fully well that they were advocating for a lifestyle and way of thinking different from the rest of the world. It is the driving force behind the creation of Stoicism and many of the philosophies of life. Philosophy is an attempt to train people to live life in a new way and see the world from a different perspective to transform them (Hadot 1995, 107). These ancient philosophers had seen a world filled with fear, anxiety, and unhappiness. They wanted to give purpose to life and transcend these negative emotions to find true happiness and tranquility. Therefore, the person who follows the path of philosophy becomes different from the world in which they live, and that world may not understand why they are the way they are.

"And nonetheless he must live this life every day, in this world in which he feels himself a stranger and in which others perceive him to be one as well." – Pierre Hadot, Philosophy as a Way of Life, pg. 58.

Think about what you have learned up to this point. The Stoics say everything the world tells us we need (money, career, family, house, material possessions, etc.) is not really important. In fact, you should be indifferent to them. They describe how desires and passions can be dangerous territory. They talk about how good and bad only exist within ourselves, and that which does not come from us is also something we must be indifferent to. What other people think of us is unimportant; all that matters is what we think of ourselves. And the only true good in life is that of virtue, with the key to happiness coming from living the pillars of Stoicism.

This is not how most of the world lives.

Which is why it is not an easy path.

But the rewards of the Stoic way can make it worth it. To live a life of more positive emotions and significantly reduced negative ones, allowing peace and tranquility to flow throughout your inner being more and more each day. Living the four pillars and thinking with a rational mind will lead to better decisions in life and less regret, which people recovering from addiction can definitely use. And you can learn to live each day to the fullest, as if it was your last, with a purpose to every moment of your existence.

These rewards are why I choose to be a Stoic.

They are what I needed in my recovery.

Epictetus gives another warning within this chapter. If you choose to live the life of a Stoic, since it is so different from the way other people live, there is a good chance that people may not understand why you are the way you are. Be content with looking foolish and dull for not knowing about all those external things on which the rest of the world focuses much of their attention. Maybe you do not know the best cryptocurrency to invest in or what stocks will take off. Perhaps you do not know the current fashion trend that everyone is following or what is happening in the entertainment world. Maybe you do not keep up with all the emerging technology or concern yourself with having a luxury car. Your focus in life lies in things greater than these externals. However, since the rest of the world places so much emphasis and value on these things, there is the chance that other people may view you as ignorant for your indifference. But remember, the reputation others give you should be of no concern, so what these people think does not matter.

Epictetus follows this by saying that you should not desire to know anything. He isn't saying that you know nothing. If you follow the path of the Stoic, wisdom is one virtue you cultivate. If the rest of the world focuses on all these external things you are indifferent to, then you should not desire to know what they do. Do not spend your energy trying to know what other people are doing or pursuing. Your pursuit of knowledge lies down a different path from theirs.

Epictetus then warns that if people see you as somebody, distrust yourself. It should be a red flag in your pursuits. Remember that you should be a stranger to the world, since you choose to be indifferent to the things they value. If you are seen as somebody to the rest of the world, it might be a sign that you are moving away from the Stoic path and moving down the one they live in. What you say and how you live are no longer strange to them; it is more familiar.

Two roads diverged in a wood, and I—
I took the one less traveled by,
And that has made all the difference.
- Robert Frost, The Road Not Taken.

Robert Frost's poem *The Road Not Taken* talks about a fork in the road with two paths to travel down. One is the way of the rest of the world that is well worn and often taken, whereas the other is rarely traveled with more plant growth, making it more challenging to traverse. And this is basically what Epictetus discusses in this chapter's last sentence. You can travel the path of the Stoic or that of the rest of the world. You cannot go down both because each path has a different goal and set of values. The more you try to live the way of the world, the less you will live as a Stoic and vice versa. To live one requires the neglect of the other. You cannot have the best of both worlds, no matter how badly you may want to try. This is the essence of Stoic courage. Do you have the strength to walk down the path that few people take, not caring what the rest of the world thinks?

"It's easy to stand with the crowd. It takes courage to stand alone."
– Mahatma Gandhi

CHAPTER 14

Only Blame Yourself
(Wisdom)

If you wish your children and your wife and your friends to live forever, you are foolish, for you wish things to be in your power which are not so, and what belongs to others to be your own. So likewise, if you wish your servant to be without fault, you are foolish, for you wish vice not to be vice but something else. – Chapter 14, Epictetus' Enchiridion.

B laming. I've done it. I'm sure you have done it. Pretty much everyone has done it in life.

Researchers in psychology have discovered this interesting habit in humans they call self-serving bias, where people can easily take credit when good things happen in life but will lay blame when things go bad (Blundell 2015). Reasons people might turn to blame others for their troubles are: it protects from feelings of vulnerability, it's easy, it unloads backed-up feelings, protects the ego, and it feeds the need for control.

Addicts can be pretty good at the blame game. I am not sure about you, but I could give dozens of reasons why it was the fault of others for why I needed to drink or use. It wasn't my fault. I had to drink because of: my work, my ex-wife, someone who died, I owed money, etc. It should be apparent why addicts often shift to using blame to explain their addictions. As I discussed earlier in the book, addicts frequently attempt to exert control over the world around them as a counterbalance to the lack of control they experience due to their addictions. Blaming others becomes a way of regaining some semblance of power in their lives. This inclination to lay blame is a natural response to the core essence of addiction—a struggle with self-control.

Long before psychologists discussed the self-serving bias, Stoics realized the fault lies solely within us and that we have the power to live in a way that we would not need to blame others again.

In this chapter, Epictetus points out that if people or events outside of our control disturb us, the only person to blame for us being bothered is ourselves. Not the other person. Not the event. In fact, he discusses you are being foolish. Irrational. Unwise. You are thinking and acting in a way that is the opposite of the Stoic virtue of wisdom. Remember, the opposites of virtue are the vices of life. And the only bad that exists in the world are the vices we allow ourselves to commit. Therefore, if you are bothered by things not going your way or beyond your control, there is nobody to blame, and the only one misbehaving at that moment is you (since you are not practicing wisdom).

Returning once again to the concept of death. It can often be a natural human reaction for us to find someone…something…maybe even God…to blame for the death of a loved one. But the harsh reality that Epictetus is pointing out is that you are the foolish one for holding on to the wish that they continue to live. You should have accepted the inevitability of their death long before and realized that it was possible every moment you were alive. Or, as he said, you are foolish since you wish for them to live forever and for something in your power that belongs to another (God, nature, the universe, chance, or whatever your higher power may be).

For the next part of this chapter, he discusses your servants' vices (faults or flaws). However, what is more helpful is to think of this from the perspective of anyone you may interact with.

It is so easy for us to get caught up in the faults or flaws of others. Have you ever been around someone and wondered why they are acting a certain way or questioned why they said something? Have you ever found yourself being emotionally disturbed by the behavior of others? Have you ever wanted someone to act in a way you think they should? If you can answer yes to any of these questions, then Epictetus says that the foolish one is you and not the other person. You were emotionally disturbed by something entirely out of your control (another person's behavior). You can't change someone else; they must be willing to change for themselves (another thing addicts know all too well).

"It is ridiculous not to escape from one's own vices, which is possible, while trying to escape the vices of others, which is impossible." – Marcus Aurelius, Meditations, 7.71.

Nobody is perfect. And that nobody includes you. It is impossible to escape from the vices of others; it is only possible to do something about your own vices. In fact, this is the essence of Step 6 and Step 7 in 12-Step based programs. If you notice, it says nothing about correcting the defects of other people's characters; it only talks about fixing your own. As Marcus Aurelius discusses above, the only vices we can escape in this world are the ones we have since we can do something about them, but trying to flee from the ones of others is impossible or foolish in Epictetus's opinion. And the worst part is we can get so fixated on correcting others rather than focusing our time and attention on ourselves. Therefore, rather than getting caught up in how other people behave and being emotionally affected by them, learn to practice acceptance and look inwards. In fact, learning not to be caught up in the faults of others is a beautiful practice in the characteristic of patience.

But if you wish not to be disappointed in your desires, that is in your own power. Exercise, therefore, what is in your power. A man's master is he who is able to confer or remove whatever that man seeks or shuns. Whoever then would be free, let him wish nothing, let him decline nothing, which depends on others; else he must necessarily be a slave. – Chapter 14, Epictetus' Enchiridion.

To have everything you desire, you need to focus on that which you control. You can have whatever you want if you choose wisely (discussed in an earlier chapter). There are people out there who have control over others. The people in power of others can give or take away whatever another person wishes to have or to avoid. An easy example would be addicts' relationships with dealers (if you ever had one). That person had something that you needed, so they were in control of you. I remember times in my cocaine addiction waiting for the dealer to call me back, having to drive at random times of the night and meet in any place they saw fit. By having what I desired and being able to give it to me, my dealer was the one in complete control of my actions. The dealer also has control through avoidance because you are trying to avoid that come down, and by having what you need to prevent it, they also exert their power in that way. Another example of avoidance I can remember in my life was when I was dealing with hangovers and trembling hands in the morning during my worst alcoholism. The liquor store was in total control of me as I waited and waited for the time for them to open so I could go down there and get what I needed to avoid that horrible feeling.

And this doesn't have to be related to only our addictions. It can be anything you desire or wish to stay away from. But you will be under their control if someone has power over these things. And as Epictetus says above, you will be a slave to them.

Returning to what I discussed earlier, desiring people to behave as we want them to and not have a vice or character flaws is hopeless. Taking a broader perspective, we become subject to the control of those we wish to change. Our emotional state becomes reliant on the actions and behavior of others. How many times have we allowed someone else's actions or words to ruin our day? In those moments, we inadvertently grant that person power over our experiences. It's essential to recognize our role in allowing external influences to affect our emotions. Blaming others or external circumstances for ruining our day is a misguided response. In truth, the responsibility lies with us for granting that power to external factors. By practicing self-awareness and taking ownership of our reactions, we gain the ability to cultivate emotional resilience and independence from the actions of others.

For me, this has been one of the most empowering realizations of practicing Stoicism. I do not have to give anyone or anything that happens power over my emotions or day. It is my choice. And these days, I live my life by choosing not to give them the power, and because of this, I have felt such a profoundly fulfilling tranquility flow through my existence.

Therefore, if you genuinely want to be free, you need to learn how to wish for nothing and decline nothing that depends on others or things outside your control. Stop being foolish and desiring things from the world (people to act how you want, freedom from death, etc.) that you must learn to accept since you have no power over them. Because the more you want things that are not within your control, the more you will be the slave to everyone and everything that has those things in their power. There is no room to blame the world or others in Stoicism; the only one to blame is ourselves for wanting something that we had no right to begin with. Mental and emotional freedom is a choice you have as long as you have the wisdom to choose wisely what you desire.

> *"Nothing in the world can bother you as much as your own mind, I tell you. In fact, others seem to be bothering you, but it is not others, it is your own mind." – Gurudev Sri Sri Ravi Shankar*

CHAPTER 15

The Feast of Life
(Justice, Temperance)

Remember that you must behave as at a banquet. Is anything brought round to you? Put out your hand and take a moderate share. Does it pass by you? Do not stop it. Is it not yet come? Do not yearn in desire toward it, but wait till it reaches you. So with regard to children, wife, office, riches; and you will some time or other be worthy to feast with the gods. And if you do not so much as take the things which are set before you, but are able even to forego them, then you will not only be worthy to feast with the gods, but to rule with them also. For, by thus doing, Diogenes and Heraclitus, and others like them, deservedly became divine and were so recognized. – Chapter 15, Epictetus' Enchiridion.

In this chapter, Epictetus uses the metaphor of life being a feast in which we are attending to discuss how we should treat the three parts of life. He illustrates this by advising on how we should act towards food that has passed by (past), food that is brought around (present), and the food that is yet to come (future). I will discuss this in a slightly different order, focusing on the past and future before concluding with the present.

"Life is divided into three parts: what was, what is and what shall be. Of these three periods, the present is short, the future is doubtful and the past alone is certain." – Seneca, On the Shortness of Life, Chapter X.

The past can be the worst enemy for anyone in recovery. Getting stuck on thoughts of the things we lost and our actions committed can be an easy trap we fall into. Relationships gone. Money thrown away. Careers destroyed. Possessions lost. Memories of the pain we caused and the harm we brought to those we care for. But as Seneca pointed out in his quote, of the three parts of life, the past is the only one that is certain. It is the only one that we cannot do anything about. Therefore, in the feast of life, the past is the food we already had a chance to consume; we need to stop thinking about it. It has already moved beyond us, and the more we focus on it, the less time we spend paying attention to the food directly in front of us.

"...but the minds of the engrossed, just as if weighted by a yoke, cannot turn and look behind. And so their life vanishes into an abyss...." – Seneca, On the Shortness of Life, Chapter X.

Seneca provides even further warning about why we must let the past move on. People with troubled minds and a bothersome past can become engrossed so much in the things they have done that their current life can vanish into an abyss of darkness. No longer are they living in the present, but now they find themselves trapped in the thoughts of what they have done, imprisoned in the days that have gone by. It is almost necessary for people like this not to look behind, to accept what has moved beyond them, and focus on now.

As for those plates yet to come (future), do not reach for them and try to force them to come to you quicker. A relationship, children, a job, money. I feel this can be something people in recovery can also find themselves doing. We sober up and begin rebuilding our lives, and the beast of instant gratification we fed during our addictions comes back to life with a loud roar within us. The relationships we destroyed need to come back to us quickly. We want to be back on track with the careers we might have destroyed. We crave financial security again after destroying any savings we might have had. Our addictions took some time to destroy our lives (for some of us, we could have been destroying things for years), so it is safe to say that it will take some time to get those things back. So do not force them to come into your life and wait for them to arrive at the proper time.

One thing that Stoics realized is that many of the negative emotions we experience are self-inflicted punishments. We feel emotions like anxiety, anger, and depression when we want things in life to come to us faster than they are arriving. We can have anger over things not going our way in sobriety. Depressed thoughts about what we lost and why it is taking so long to get it back. Anxiety over what the future holds and what will happen to us. There are so many stories of relapse that you can come across where someone gave in to their addictions because they found that life was not going the way they had wanted at the time and things were not improving fast enough. So, they fall back into that old pattern of needing relief from these negative emotions, and using has always been the quickest way to achieve that relief. Therefore, we mustn't focus on the food coming toward us because we lose ourselves thinking about that and torturing our minds on when it will arrive.

The last point on the future to discuss comes from the Seneca quote at the beginning of the chapter. The future is doubtful. We do not know what will happen or what will come our way. Prepare yourself for the possibility that the things you are waiting to come in front of you to feast on may never make it to you. Accept the reality that you may never get back the things you lost, and you may never get the things you are waiting for. You may not even live to see the end of this day. So, you must always enjoy the things in your life that are in front of you and that you have right now within your grasp.

What should you do when the food (opportunities) comes to rest before you? How should we handle the present moment in which we live? Seneca discussed that this is the shortest part of life, which is why we need to live in the moment. If we find ourselves caught up in the past and the future, we may find life's opportunities passing us by because we ignored them when they were before us. So, live in the now to see what you have before you because it will quickly become what is past.

But what do we do with these opportunities?

Epictetus advises it is acceptable to have your share but do it in moderation. When you have food finally passed to you, the more you take for yourself, the less there is for others. It is a Stoic reminder to live a life of moderation that also considers other people (temperance and justice).

Now, as people in recovery, we know we cannot partake in certain things. However, we also need to practice moderation in everything we do in life; we do not want to transfer our addictions to other aspects of our lives. For example, are you in a relationship? That is wonderful, but do not get to the point of codependency, since this is unhealthy for you or the person you are with. Do you have a good job? That is even better, but do not become a workaholic where your life is entirely your job since this robs time away from the people you care about. Enjoy food again (I know I found this in my recovery). Enjoy, but do not replace your previous addictions with food. The central concept is that in anything and everything you do, you need to do it in moderation. Too much of anything (even things that might be good for you) can harm you physically or mentally. And as you do something, think about other people in your life and society. Are your actions taking others into consideration, or are they selfish?

Epictetus finishes his metaphor with the ultimate way to participate in this feast of life. If you can do the other three things, you are on a path to a healthier mental state and a better life. However, if you can work towards this level, you can hit a deeply enlightened way of living.

Can you gain the ability not to partake in the things in front of you?

Just because an opportunity presents itself does not mean you have to participate. Yes, you may desire to be in a relationship, but is that the right one for you? Is that job going to be healthy for you to have? Will taking part in a particular event be good for you? Just because an opportunity arises (food is placed in front of you) does not mean you have to consume it, even if it is in moderation. To truly master the feast and reach the ultimate level is to hit that point in life where you can reject things, even though they might look like something you would want. I think this becomes an important goal for us to strive towards in recovery. Sometimes the things we want in life might not be suitable for our recovery and could put us in danger of losing it.

The feast of life.

The past, present, and future.

The Stoics realized that to keep our thoughts trained on the past and the future is useless since one is certain and the other is in doubt. They also discovered that they cause many negative emotions we feel in life by our minds focusing on these two aspects of time. So, keep your thoughts and focus on the present moment since we need to be ready for what comes before us in this short time. However, we need to remember to practice moderation and consideration of others at the same time. And always remember that even though an opportunity may come knocking on your door, it does not mean you have to answer it if it will not be something good for you.

Live a life worthy of being seated at the divine feast.

"The future hasn't happened yet and the past is gone. So I think the only moment we have is right here and now, and I try to make the best of those moments, the moments that I'm in." - Annie Lennox

CHAPTER 16

The Grief of Others
(Justice, Temperance, Wisdom)

When you see anyone weeping in grief because his son has gone abroad, or is dead, or because he has suffered in his affairs, take care not to be overcome by the apparent evil, but discriminate and be ready to say, "What hurts this man is not this occurrence itself—for another man might not be hurt by it—but the view he chooses to take of it." As far as conversation goes, however, do not disdain to accommodate yourself to him and, if need be, to groan with him. Take heed, however, not to groan inwardly, too. – Chapter 16, Epictetus' Enchiridion.

---

5 6 million people die each year in the world. That is over 153,000 daily, 6,300 each hour, 106 each minute, and almost 2 people a second (Medindia n.d.). This can vary year by year and source by source, but the number is staggeringly high no matter what. This also means that death is something that is constantly happening across the world every single day.

In earlier chapters, Epictetus discussed ways to prepare to deal with loss in our own lives. But how should you handle your interactions with other people who may suffer from some form of loss? Throughout life, people with whom you have some relationship (family, friends, coworkers, etc.) will have to deal with their own loss. And this does not have to be only the death of someone they care for; it could also be things like children moving away from home or other forms of loss (unemployment, financial issues, relationships ending, etc.).

The first thing that Epictetus reminds you of in this chapter is what your education in Stoicism has taught you to this point. It is not the event itself that is causing this person to have grief, but it is how they choose to judge the event that has happened. And most likely, the cause of their loss is something that is out of their control. However, there is a good chance that this person is not a Stoic like yourself, which means they may not have the same perspective you have gained on events from which they are suffering.

Knowing that Stoics see the world differently than most people, they realize that sometimes we might have to talk or act as if we agree with conventional values, treating what we have learned to be indifferent to as being good or bad (Robertson 2018, 105). And this idea is the core concept Epictetus discusses in this chapter. In certain situations, we may have to say things or act in ways that may not truly represent our Stoic view of life.

Why would Epictetus recommend this?

Remember, one of the core virtues of Stoicism is justice. Therefore, we must be considerate of others when we interact with them. Think of someone dealing with grief over the death of a loved one. Would it be right for you to talk to that person and tell them they have to accept it and that only their judgments are giving them grief, and they should learn to be just indifferent to it? They are not Stoic, which would make it just cruel to drop all of this on them during their grief. Epictetus is pointing out that the right thing to do in this situation would be to accommodate them in your conversations with them. Listen. Understand their grief. If they need someone to cry with, then be that person who they can cry with. Doing the right thing in interacting with someone suffering in grief is not to lecture them on Stoic philosophy; it is not the right time. Instead, be there for them, understand them, and give them what they need to help them through the moment.

While outwardly sharing in someone else's grief, Epictetus warns that it is crucial to avoid internalizing their emotions. As a Stoic, you understand the significance of approaching life's events with indifference and acceptance, even as you empathize with others' losses.

Later in the book, Epictetus will discuss the most effective ways to reveal and discuss the Stoic philosophy you choose to live by. However, he emphasizes the necessity of doing so at the appropriate time and place. When someone is grappling with grief, it is not the right moment for such discussions. Instead, being a good person means providing them the support they need to navigate their sorrow. This compassionate and empathetic response is the right thing to do.

"Love and compassion are necessities, not luxuries. Without them humanity cannot survive." – Dalai Lama

CHAPTER 17

The Universal Play
(Courage)

Remember that you are an actor in a drama of such sort as the Author chooses—if short, then in a short one; if long, then in a long one. If it be his pleasure that you should enact a poor man, or a cripple, or a ruler, or a private citizen, see that you act it well. For this is your business— to act well the given part, but to choose it belongs to another. – Chapter 17, Epictetus' Enchiridion.

In a previous chapter, Epictetus used the concept of a feast to discuss how we should view and behave regarding our past, present, and future. Now he uses the metaphor of a play (a movie or television show could also be used) to discuss the true nature of acceptance and being the best person we can be, no matter what situation or conditions we confront. Do you have the courage to accept what life presents you with and live to the best of your ability? Or will you complain about a perception of unfairness from the world?

He first points out that you are not the writer of this play... movie...TV show. Depending on your belief system, the writer of this world or universe could be God, your Higher Power, or simply Nature itself. But the obvious point is that it is not you. And there are things in your life that this writer will decide that you have no choice but to accept. We do not get to choose how significant our role will be, whether it will be a small part (we die prematurely) or an extended part (we live to old age). We do not get to choose the time our role spends acting in this grand universal play, which is a further reminder of the Stoic view that urges an acceptance of death as an inevitability and something that can come to any of us at any given moment.

Are we given the role of someone who must deal with a physical or mental disability (crippled)? It is not like a person chooses these conditions; as discussed earlier in this book, things like these are out of our control. I remember the depression I experienced upon discovering that I was bipolar, as I thought it was unfair that I had to deal with this mental condition while so many other people did not have to. However, I would discover that it is only through accepting and embracing the mental disorder that I will live life to the best of my capabilities. We can hold this same view for the addictions that we suffer from. We do not choose to live the role of an addict. We can try to run from it, hide from it, or complain about it, but it will not change the reality of our situation. Only through accepting the fact that we are addicts will we be able to live a life of recovery.

We do not have the choice of the positions in life we are born into. Being born into poverty, middle class, or wealth is not something we choose. We do not even decide the country where our life begins, which could have dramatic differences in what poverty and wealth can look and feel like. And depending on what country you are born into, there can be considerable differences in the ability of upward mobility, which is the ability to change your living conditions. In some places of the world, you can start as a poor person and end up wealthy, whereas, in other areas, this could be a nearly impossible task. And even if you find yourself born into a place in which it is possible, much of what would allow you to change your position in life would depend on several forces outside your control, so you need to learn to accept that it may or may never happen.

I think this concept goes well with this universal play concept. Actors can audition for the parts which they desire to play. They can show off their skills and what they may have learned through other parts. But it is ultimately up to someone else whether they will get that part or be cast for another. William Shakespeare would again expand on this quote from Epictetus in one of his plays.

"All the world's a stage, and all the men and women merely players: they have their exits and their entrances; and one man in his time plays many parts…" – William Shakespeare, As You Like It (Act 2, Scene 7).

Shakespeare points out that in this grand universal play, we are cast to actually play several parts. You might play the roles of son or daughter, father or mother, aunt or uncle, grandfather or grandmother. Some people may be born into families with two parents, others just one, and others may have no parents. You might have siblings or be the only child. Some people will find themselves capable of having children, while others may have to accept that they cannot have any. These are not choices we are given but are written for us by this grand Author.

You could also be cast to be a friend, coworker, server, manager, soldier, or fellow citizen. The roles of this universal play are countless when you think of all the ways in which we interact with other people on this planet daily. No matter what path you live in this world, you will constantly play different roles to a variety of people.

"Life's like a play. It's not the length but the excellence of the acting that matters." – Seneca

How will you perform your roles in this grand universal play? Are you going to accept what you have been cast for, or will you complain that it is not the role you wanted? I think the metaphor of a play (movie or TV show) is perfect for life. How many movies have you watched where some of the acting was terrible, but there was that one person who played their role so well they stuck out and shined? One excellent actor can turn an intolerable movie into something worth sitting through.

You were chosen for the roles you have in your life right now by the grand Author of all that happens. You need to ask yourself what it would require for you to perform these roles to the best of your abilities. Do not think or care about how other people perform in this play; the quality of their performance is up to them. All that matters is the quality of yours. Accept and be honored that the grand Author has given the roles you were cast for; there is a reason you have been. And now, do your part in making sure that you make this universal play one worth watching through the performance you bring to it.

You are special.

It is why you were chosen for this play.

Now let's see what you can do with what you have been given.

"In the end, we are not the roles we play. We are the light that animates every soul in the dance we call life." – Alan Cohen

CHAPTER 18

There Is No Such Thing as Bad Luck
(Wisdom)

When a raven happens to croak unluckily, be not overcome by appearances, but discriminate and say, "Nothing is portended to me, either to my paltry body, or property, or reputation, or children, or wife. But to me all portents are lucky if I will. For whatsoever happens, it belongs to me to derive advantage therefrom." – Chapter 18, Epictetus' Enchiridion.

The raven has long been considered one of the most intelligent birds. Because of this, it has served symbolically in various ways throughout human history. Sometimes thought of as a sign of loss or a bad omen—other times of prophecy and insight. In the example above, you can see a blending of these two meanings, where the raven is one of prophecy and insight but also serves as a bad omen.

Whether or not you have thought of the raven as a sign of bad luck, people hold plenty of other superstitions. It could be a black cat, a broken mirror, opening an umbrella inside the house, Friday the 13th, or having to knock on wood. Or, even if you do not believe in superstitions, you may have said at some point that you or someone else were experiencing bad luck.

But luck is not the point Epictetus is trying to get at here.

Bad things that happen do not happen to you.

This chapter is another Stoic reminder of the true essence of who you are; your character. You are not your body, what you own, the reputation people choose to give you, and not even your children or partner. When bad things happen in life, they happen to things that are not your character. It might be harmful to your body, loss of property, damage to your reputation, or something to your family. However, nothing in life can damage your character unless you give it the power to do so. It is your choice if you allow "bad" (remember the Stoic view on good or bad) things that happen to change the person you are.

Many of us in our addictions learn perfectly well how to play the victim. We even become masters of it. We find so many ways to blame all the bad things in our lives on others or simply on life being unfair. The irony, of course, is that much of the bad luck we had in our lives was from our own doing. Of course, bad things will happen when you commit devious and horrendous actions. Therefore, in our sobriety, it becomes necessary that we stop playing the victim and take accountability for the bad things we have caused and may still cause in our own lives.

This does not mean that "bad" things won't continue to happen now that you are in recovery and making better decisions. Knowing that most of the world lies in a realm beyond our control suggests that unwanted events will continue to occur. As the saying goes...shit happens. But it is your choice in the damage you will allow it to do. Are you going to let these moments harm your recovery and your character? Who you are is your ultimate possession, and it is within your choice to decide if you will allow the "bad" things in life to damage that because only you can let that happen.

Epictetus finishes this passage with something that he has touched on earlier. He discusses how he sees no such thing as bad omens or bad luck. He sees all of it as being lucky. Whatever happens in life is in your control to turn it into an advantage. This goes back to the discussion of the concept of the Stoic challenge. Even when adversity strikes, and it seems like "bad luck" might be upon you, this presents the perfect opportunity for you to strengthen your character. Realize that whatever is happening is happening to things outside your control and that it allows you to grow as a person. We can see everything as being lucky (good luck) if we can turn it into a learning and character development opportunity.

How would it feel to be lucky every day?

The choice is yours right now.

"You never can tell whether bad luck may not after all turn out to be good luck." – Winston Churchill

CHAPTER 19

Become Unconquerable
(Courage, Temperance, Wisdom)

You can be unconquerable if you enter into no combat in which it is not in your own power to conquer. When, therefore, you see anyone eminent in honors or power, or in high esteem on any other account, take heed not to be bewildered by appearances and to pronounce him happy; for if the essence of good consists in things within our own power, there will be no room for envy or emulation. But, for your part, do not desire to be a general, or a senator, or a consul, but to be free; and the only way to this is a disregard of things which lie not within our own power. – Chapter 19, Epictetus' Enchiridion.

Going into combat, not from a militaristic point of view but one in which we are fighting for a desired outcome, can be common among those dealing with addiction. I think we become quite good at finding reasons to fight. Not just physically but verbally, too. Much of this probably stems from the earlier discussion on how addicts exert a sphere of control over the world and the surrounding people to deal with the lack of control they might feel from their addictions. I can easily think back to the many times when I was in the depths of my addiction where I would get into verbal arguments with people because I needed my view expressed and wanted things how I wanted them to be.

The world had to bend to my view and my will.

I also discussed earlier in the book that we need to learn not to be this way in our recovery and discover ways to accept life and release this need to control. I think this is why anger management is so commonly found in recovery programs, as they teach us how to stop fighting and learn to control our emotions.

But does this mean no more combat for us?

It might seem to you at this point that Stoics would view being combative as something that a person should not do. But they understood it is impossible to envision a life in which we will no longer have any battles. It is just not the way that the world works. Disagreements and adversity are common to everyone in daily living. For those of us in recovery, we may have left a massive path of destruction in the wake of our addictions that might cause many battles that we have to face now in sobriety. We might even have people who want to get revenge on us for what we have done. And even if we get through all these past issues, it is not like the world will suddenly be perfect, and we won't face further battles as we navigate the rest of our lives.

In this chapter, Epictetus almost speaks to this old, addict way of thinking. He is talking about how we can still face challenges and combat while continuing to have things the way we want them to be. Even in the first sentence, he describes we can become unconquerable in combat. That there is a way in which we could always win. We can still have things the way we want them to be, much like how it was when we were in our addictions. However, he explains one caveat in this chapter that we need to follow to make this possible.

We need to choose our battles wisely.

Hopefully, by this point in the book, you have begun to understand that when the Stoics discuss the concept of acceptance, they are looking at things that are truly outside of our control. It is not an opinion. It is a fact. It is just how the world is. When we tried to exert our control over the world during our addictions, we tried to control things that were not under our power. And the more that we tried to force things to our will, the more destruction it would cause when they came crashing down. This concept is like when we throw a ball into the air. We try to challenge and overcome the force of gravity, but the higher we push that ball upwards, the harder and faster it will come right back down at us.

So how do we choose our battles wisely?

When faced with a problem or confrontation, you need to ask yourself what aspects of it are within your power. When you enter this battle, what should you be fighting for as a result? You first must accept that you do not have control over people, places, or things (as they say in recovery), so outcomes that relate to those aspects of the battle cannot be your goal. However, you have control over the character that you bring to the struggle and what you can gain as a person from the confrontation.

Let me give an example of how I have used this concept in my life. As an addict, I wanted people to think how I wanted them to or do things I wanted them to do. And if I could not change them, I would resent them for not being the way I want them to be (and maybe even devise a way to get revenge on them). But I do not have control over another person, how they are, and how they act. However, I control how I perceive or interact with them. Therefore, I changed the battle from wanting to alter someone to how I want them to be and resenting them if they do not comply to now accepting them for who they are (flaws and all). It became about patience and understanding within myself. I made the battle solely about myself and how I will think of them in my mind and in my interactions. The battle went from outside of me to inside. I can win that battle because that is something entirely under my control.

What does this mean for the battles that you cannot win? This is where you must learn how to practice acceptance. As the Serenity Prayer says, you must accept the things you cannot change. And a battle you cannot win is essentially something that you cannot change.

The rest of this chapter discusses specific examples of battles that you could have with others and how to deal with them. Epictetus focuses on envy and jealousy since these are strong negative emotions that can often lead to others, such as anger. They can also cause you to create battles that may have never existed. Sometimes when we see a person with something we want, we can start hatching schemes on how we could get it (or a part of it) or start thinking negative thoughts about how we would like to see them lose it. It is almost like seeing someone living a better life than our own can cause us to look at our own lives and what we have. And if we are not happy with our situation, it makes us miserable for not having what they have.

Bitterness.

Envy.

But are those thoughts that we have genuinely with merit?

Epictetus points out that just because you see someone has money, power, and is held up in high esteem, does not mean that they are happy. Earlier in the book, I discussed how studies find that wealthy people and countries suffer from higher levels of depression and anxiety. Just because someone appears to have more than you in life materialistically, it does not necessarily translate to them being better off than you are mentally and internally. The grass is always greener on the other side. It is almost human nature for a person to see another person having more and then assume that their life must be better. But more often than not, that is not true. Besides, if the goal in life is to be proud of who you are and have a virtuous character, would envy and jealousy be the signs of a good person? And I know that these can be natural emotions that are hard to combat. As with many parts of this philosophy, it is easier said than done. I will share an example from my life of how I faced the essence of this chapter.

I had been practicing Stoicism for quite some time when this situation came upon me. Someone who is very near and dear to me in life was able to get a job that paid more money than I could ever imagine. Life was going well for him, and everything was going in the right direction. As this happened in his life, I was still in a small room at my sober living and unemployed because of the pandemic. So, when I heard about his new job and how much he would make, I felt this deep jealousy over what he had and how his life was going for him.

It also made me see where my life was and how I had nothing of what he had.

I felt that envy strongly, but I confronted it. The battle I could win was in how I perceived the situation. I was getting envious of a person I cared for a lot. I reminded myself how hard he had worked to get to the place in life that he was in. How this new job and the money that came with it was a reward for years of hard work that he had dedicated himself to. He is a good person who deserves to live a good life. So, I should not be jealous; I should be happy for him. And as I came to these realizations, I found those negative feelings disappeared and replaced with happiness for him in how his life was going.

The other fascinating part of this situation was seeing that "grass is always greener" playing out with him. Yes, he was making more money. Yes, he could buy and do more things. But I also noticed the stress and anxiety he was going through because of his new job. The sacrifice of more money and a higher position meant it had to increase its internal cost. Just because life was going in the right direction did not mean that everything was perfect. Yes, I might have been unemployed and living in a small room, but stress and anxiety were completely absent in my life.

This is the last part of what Epictetus was saying in this chapter. A good person should not be envious, and the path to achieving this is within all our control. You should not wish for money, property, or prestige in life. You should want to be a person who feels free. One of the great ironies in life is that even people with money and power can become jealous of people with even more money, power, and nicer things. Sometimes the rich try to even out rich each other. Have the best art, the nicest house, the best yacht, and a rare car.

So how can any and everyone be free?

To release your desires for things outside of you (externals) and out of your control. I may not have a lot of things in life, materialistically wise. But what I do have is peace of mind and tranquility. I live a good life, am a good person, and try to do the right thing each day that I live. I have felt that feeling of freedom. Now when I see people with more things than me (money, property, and prestige), I think it's good for them, but I also can't help but notice the cost to them mentally and wonder if it is worth it. Ultimately, I realized that a good person does not feel envy or jealousy because a good person knows what truly is valuable in life. And the most valuable thing can be owned by anyone at any moment; it is a choice within your grasp and control.

Nobody likes to lose in battle. It leads to frustration, anger, anxiety, and other negative emotions (which can be triggers for some of us). However, choosing your battles wisely and only those in your control will have positive results throughout your life, leading to tranquility, peace, and an absence of anger.

Therefore, choose wisely and never lose again.

"Though one may conquer a thousand times a thousand men in battle, yet he indeed is the noblest victor who conquers himself." –Buddha, Dhammapada verse, 104-105.

CHAPTER 20

Anger Is a Choice
(Justice, Temperance, Wisdom)

Remember that it is not he who gives abuse or blows, who affronts, but the view we take of these things as insulting. When, therefore, anyone provokes you, be assured that it is your own opinion which provokes you. Try, therefore, in the first place, not to be bewildered by appearances. For if you once gain time and respite, you will more easily command yourself. – Chapter 20, Epictetus' Enchiridion.

S toics often talk about anger as they realize it is one of the most destructive of passions and human emotions.

"We must here encounter with the most dangerous, intractable, and brutal of passions; the most unmannerly and loathsome, as well as ridiculous; to conquer this monster will do much towards the establishment of human peace." – Seneca, On Anger, pg. 1.

It is an emotion that directly contradicts and threatens the Stoic virtue of justice. And if we need to keep our minds rational to make the right decisions to become the good person we want to be, then something must be done about the anger that can erupt inside us. In our moments of anger and rage, we find ourselves not thinking right and doing or saying things we would not usually want to do. How many times have you had to apologize or make amends for something you said or did because you were irrationally thinking with an angry mind? Even the Big Book of Alcoholics Anonymous states:

> "If we were to live, we had to be free of anger." – Alcoholics Anonymous (Big Book) - Page 66.

Many of us in our addictions lived lives filled with anger and resentment. And often, we use that anger and resentment to fuel our addictions. It gave us reasons to consume our drug of choice. Therefore, in our recovery, we need to learn to reduce the anger we feel in our lives, not only to avoid possible triggers to relapse but to grow into a new way of living and thinking differently from our old addict ways.

People will say or do things to you that might provoke anger. It is not like it is something that will ever disappear; it is a part of you. Buddhists believe everyone always has good and bad seeds within themselves (our good and bad characteristics). However, it is our choice which seeds we choose to water and grow.

So, what do you do if someone is saying or doing something to provoke your anger?

How can you grow the good seed?

As with so many other parts of this book, Epictetus points out that it is not the event itself that is the issue; it is how we choose to judge that event. What the person is saying or doing is not you; that is solely on them. It is their own minds and impulses that guide their actions and words. However, how you view those words or actions is your own judgment. And how you decide to judge those things will determine the seed you choose to water and the emotion you will let out from it.

> *"When another blames you or hates you, or people voice similar criticisms, go to their souls, penetrate inside and see what sort of people they are. You will realize that there is no need to be racked with anxiety that they should hold any particular opinion about you."* – Marcus Aurelius, Meditations 9:27.

Consider the source.

If somebody you know says something that offends you (whether it be blame, hatred, or criticism), think of the person they are. Think of what you know about them and their character. When you consider the type of person they are, you might realize that their words are from their own flawed perceptions and have no bearing on who you are or have any merit for them to say what they are saying. And if the person is a stranger you have just come across, then you know perfectly well that they have no clue what they are talking about if they say anything bad about you.

One of the most valuable things I learned through Stoicism was considering the source of what people say about me. This basically comes in two forms:

1. You trust that person's opinion, and even though their criticism might be harsh, it is there to help you and should be gladly accepted and listened to in order to learn and improve. For some of us, this can be the experience we feel from a sponsor or mentor in recovery.
2. You do not trust the person's opinion, so whatever they say about you does not matter, which means there is no reason to get angry.

What do you do if it isn't what someone said but something they did that will cause you anger? Well, what they do will only cause anger and the situation to escalate if you choose to respond and allow it to. Prolonged anger is a choice that a person makes. And because it is a choice, you can also choose not to allow it.

I can think of the first situation in which I truly realized this. Road rage is a terrible expression of anger that many people (addicts or not) deal with. It leads to fights and sometimes even murder. I had been driving down the street with my daughter, and apparently, going the speed limit was not fast enough for the person behind me. So, they honked their horn at me several times, drove up next to me, flipped me off, then passed me up and cut me off. I was slightly bothered because this person did this with my young daughter in the passenger seat next to me. But the only thing I thought about at that moment was, "wow, it must suck to be that person and have so much anger." They drove off, and I had a wonderful time with my daughter. Now, if I had acted out or gotten angry, I could easily say that a good portion of my time with my daughter would have been ruined.

"When you wake up in the morning, tell yourself: The people I deal with today will be meddling, ungrateful, arrogant, dishonest, jealous, and surly. They are like this because they can't tell good from evil. But I have seen the beauty of good, and the ugliness of evil, and have recognized that the wrongdoer has a nature related to my own—not of the same blood or birth, but the same mind, and possessing a share of the divine. And so none of them can hurt me. No one can implicate me in ugliness. Nor can I feel angry at my relative, or hate him. We were born to work together like feet, hands, and eyes, like the two rows of teeth, upper and lower. To obstruct each other is unnatural. To feel anger at someone, to turn

your back on him: these are obstructions."– Marcus Aurelius, Meditations, 2:1.

Earlier in the book, I mentioned the first part of this quote when I discussed how Stoics felt that we should expect the expected when it comes to how we approach our daily lives. I had described how Marcus Aurelius would mentally prepare himself for the day by thinking of the kind of people he should expect to encounter. I wanted to circle back to this passage and give you the rest of what he said so you could see that he did not think this way out of pessimism over others but did this from a perspective of understanding and justice.

People rarely do things without reason; they generally do things they see as being beneficial to themselves, even though it might be ultimately wrong. Think of things you may have done in your addiction that you knew might have been wrong, but you may have done them anyways since you saw benefit in doing so by feeding the beast of addiction that thrived within. So, when you see someone saying or doing something that could be seen as wrong, rather than being angry, feel bad for them because they might be lost and cannot tell good from evil.

Marcus Aurelius also reminds us about the concept of Stoic justice when dealing with people who could anger us. We need to remind ourselves that we are here on this planet in our shared human experience and that we are here for the benefit of each other. And that feelings of anger towards another person will become just an obstacle in the path of us working together. Anger and cooperation do not work well together.

So even with all this knowledge, what can you do if someone angers you?

"The first motion of anger is in truth involuntary...the second deliberates." – Seneca, On Anger, pg. 5.

It is impossible to think that you can live an entire life without having someone or something stir a bit of anger inside of you. As I said earlier, we always have the seeds of good and evil inside us. In this quote, Seneca points out that we have no control over that first moment when someone does something that stirs up anger. It is involuntary. It is like a reflex reaction to that moment.

However, we have control over what we do next.

After that first reflex reaction, our mind thinks about how we are going to respond. It is within our grasp whether we will let it continue and get carried away with it or allow it to be let go. Therefore, Epictetus says that if we can just give ourselves some time, a moment to breathe, think, and not be carried away with it, we can have a better chance of having command over our response.

Basically, we need a moment to get past that first involuntary reaction.

During that moment in which you try not to get carried away with anger, it can help to think about all the other things that were discussed in this chapter. Consider the source of what caused that involuntary action to arise. Understand that only your judgment of what has been said or occurred matters. Remember that we must accept what we cannot control. Remind yourself of Stoic justice and our common bonds with all humans.

But mainly, just take a breath and let it pass.

Count to ten, as it is often recommended.

Anger is a destructive emotion; no real good ever comes from it. We must live free of anger in our sobriety since it was often a big part of our addiction. It is our choice what will happen when it comes, and we need to start making the right choices in recovery.

"For every minute you are angry you lose sixty seconds of happiness." – Ralph Waldo Emerson

CHAPTER 21

Premeditation of Trouble
(Courage, Temperance, Wisdom)

Let death and exile, and all other things which appear terrible, be daily before your eyes, but death chiefly; and you will never entertain an abject thought, nor too eagerly covet anything. – Chapter 21, Epictetus' Enchiridion.

In this chapter, Epictetus returns to *premeditatio malorum* (premeditation of troubles) and some of its benefits. I had also previously described this as being sometimes called negative visualization because it involves taking a moment to imagine losing (negative) the things we have.

Epictetus says we should have death, exile, and anything terrible that could happen in our minds daily. He says death (our own and others) first because this is the worst-case scenario for what we can experience in life. And I know that exile (being forced to leave our native country) is something that we rarely experience any longer since it is not a common practice these days. However, many of the ancient Stoics (Epictetus, Seneca, Musonius Rufus, and others) dealt with exile since the rulers of their countries often found their words and popularity to be a threat to their power.

But when I think about it, some of us in recovery have experienced a form of exile. The destructiveness of our addictions may have led to our friends and family telling us we are no longer welcome at their houses or in their lives. We may have ended up homeless after losing the opportunity to stay at the place we call home. I even had a friend at my sober living that was banned by the courts from stepping foot on his mother's property because of bringing drugs into the neighborhood (and he discovered this already a couple of years into his sobriety). So even though it may not be a common practice to be exiled from your own country, some of us know that feeling of being banned from certain places.

> *"It is in times of security that the spirit should be preparing itself to deal with difficult times; while fortune is bestowing favors on it then is the time for it to be strengthened against her rebuffs. In the midst of peace the soldier carries out maneuvers...."* – Seneca, *Letters from a Stoic, Letter 18.*

With so many things in life being out of our control, the Stoics realized we must always prepare ourselves for the possibility of "bad" things happening or misfortunes. And it is best to prepare so that we are mentally ready for them in case they happen. In the way Seneca describes above, soldiers prepare for war in times of peace. It is not like the military starts training and getting ready for battle only when war appears; it is a constant preparation that they do. Many soldiers throughout the history of the world prepared for war to find themselves never in that situation.

But at least they were prepared.

We need to think of our lives in the same fashion. We must constantly train ourselves to prepare for misfortune and adversity so that we are ready to meet them with a rational mind and clear-headedness. It is a lot more challenging to handle misfortune if you wait for yourself to be in the middle of it to figure out what you will do.

In this chapter, Epictetus suggests training your mind to think about what you would do if misfortune came into your life. Think of worst-case scenarios that could happen in the future based on the situation that you are living in now. What would you do in response to these situations if they were to happen? Like soldiers preparing for different scenarios and actions during war, you are readying your mind for how you will handle various misfortunes you can face. Invite these unpleasant thoughts of possible futures into your mind to strengthen yourself, understanding that such things may never even occur. Recent psychological research has shown that people who can accept unpleasant thoughts and feelings without being overwhelmed by them are more resilient than people who try to distract themselves or avoid such experiences (Robertson 2018, 144).

With this understanding, you can see how the premeditation of trouble can be significant to those who have suffered from addiction. One common characteristic of addicts is that we often use our drug of choice to escape unpleasant thoughts and feelings. This means in our sobriety, we need to learn how to handle them differently. And premeditation of misfortune is an exercise that is solely designed to do this for us. As a result, we become battle ready for whatever life will throw at us.

So how does it work and help?

At the time of writing this, I am living in a small bedroom at a sober living with some possessions in my life. I have a car. A bookshelf filled with books. A range of clothing to wear. A TV and a record player with a small collection of records. Is it a lot? Well, if I look back at other moments in my life…not really. I can remember times when I had so much more.

I also can remember… my last bottom, when I had only the clothes I was wearing.

All that I had funneled down to just that.

I had become an exile in the lives of everyone I knew.

When I practice premeditation of troubles (negative visualization), I think of the bad things that could bring me back to this point in life—losing everything I have with only the clothes I am wearing as all I own. Of course, my addictions have brought me to that point before, but there are many scenarios where that could happen again other than if I just relapsed (although it is a good reminder of why I need to be sober).

It happened once.

It could happen again.

And I survived it. I found a way to survive with no place to call home. I found a way to survive with no car to get around. I found a way to survive with only the clothes I wore. It is not the ideal situation that I want to be in. But I made it through. By reminding myself of this worst-case scenario, I worry less about my present life and have less anxiety over the future. This is because I know what could happen, and I know what to do to survive since I have already lived through it. And as Epictetus says in this chapter, doing this reduces any abject (miserable) thoughts, and I do not covet the things I possess. I am glad to have them, but I do not need them.

I have learned to use this kind of practice in any situation that I have in life. I think about what I will do if none of the jobs I have applied to come through. I plan what will happen if my IRS debt does not work in my favor. I ponder what steps I will take if I cannot find a publisher for this book. I think of the things in life that I am working towards or have and plan my response in case misfortune comes to me. So, when things have not worked out as I had wanted them to, such as numerous job rejections, I already have a plan for what I will do now that it has happened.

> "The Stoics weren't advocating that we dwell on how things could be worse; that would be a recipe for misery. Instead, what we should do is periodically have flickering thoughts about how our lives and circumstances could be worse." – William B. Irvine, The Stoic Challenge, pg. 78.

It is not like the Stoics are telling you to sit around every day imagining all these horrible things that might happen to your life. However, they think that doing this occasionally can positively benefit your life. A higher level of gratefulness for what you have, less anxiety over the future, and greater resiliency to deal with misfortune if it comes your way are some of the significant goals of premeditation of trouble.

The time to prepare for battle is now.

> "If you train worst case scenarios consistently, they will no longer be worst case scenarios." – Rener Gracie

CHAPTER 22
Stay Focused Despite the Naysayers
(Courage, Justice)

If you have an earnest desire toward philosophy, prepare yourself from the very first to have the multitude laugh and sneer, and say, "He is returned to us a philosopher all at once"; and, "Whence this supercilious look?" Now, for your part, do not have a supercilious look indeed, but keep steadily to those things which appear best to you, as one appointed by God to this particular station. For remember that, if you are persistent, those very persons who at first ridiculed will afterwards admire you. But if you are conquered by them, you will incur a double ridicule. – Chapter 22, Epictetus' Enchiridion.

———————

The first time I read this passage, it did not mean much to me since I was early into studying Stoicism (about two or three months). Back then, I had thought there could be nothing wrong with studying philosophy, so why would people think anything negative about the fact that you are? But now, coming back to it years later and thinking about how this philosophy has played out in my life, I understand why Epictetus had to discuss this with his students.

Therefore, for this chapter, I will explain its meaning mainly through the example of what happened to me.

When I finally told people I was reading about this philosophy called Stoicism that I had come across, they met me with three different responses. Some people were genuinely interested and asked me what it was. They may have heard a little about it or not at all, but they wondered what it was all about. It bothered other people. They confused the word Stoic with stoic. This is a common misconception. A Stoic person (capital S) is one who studies the philosophy, while a stoic person (lowercase s) is a person who shows little emotion. These individuals became concerned that I was dedicating my life to one of lack of emotion (by this point, you should realize Stoics focused on dealing with negative emotions to allow for more positive ones). I even had one family member worried I would worship Zeus (yes, some mention Zeus, but he was the god for their time and society and is not a requirement for the philosophy). The third group had this kind of reaction that could be characterized by this "Oh, you are one of those people now." Here is this guy who is an alcoholic and an addict, and now he is studying philosophy. I even had a friend, literally minutes before writing this chapter, send me a text with a meme that said, "I'm coming over. You better not be romanticizing dead heroes of Rome again." It is this third group of people that Epictetus discusses in this chapter because they have the greatest ability to push you off track on your journey as a philosopher.

One of the fascinating things about finally studying and dedicating myself to philosophy is to realize the role that it has become in the world. Here we have a subject devoted to studying who we are, why we are the way we are, how we relate to the world, and what we truly value. It is a subject that tries to get at the deeper meaning of life. Yet, the study of philosophy has been pushed to the fringe of our learning experience. As a result, many people face the possibility that they may never even take a class or learn about the subject. And if you ask me, I think it is pushing philosophy to this fringe of the learning experience that can make people ridicule those who study it.

So be prepared.

When you tell people about studying philosophy, there is a chance they might laugh at you or make fun of you. Maybe they see it as entirely useless to study or that they think you are trying to behave like you are educated and acting superior to them (supercilious).

Now, two of the Stoic virtues that you will incorporate into your life will get you through interactions with these people. First, Stoic justice reminds you that humanity is a big family navigating through life daily. Never feel or act like you are superior to others because we are all equals in the grand play of the universe. And Stoic courage has taught you that you must keep focused on doing what is right, no matter what anyone else has to say about it. That is why Epictetus says in this chapter that you never have that supercilious look or appearance and that you need to keep steady on the path of what you know is good for you. In time, many of the people that may have had an issue with your studying philosophy will admire you for the changes that it has made in the manner in which you live.

What is discussed in this chapter is very similar to the Big Book when it says:

> "To some people we need not, and probably should not emphasize the spiritual feature on our first approach. We might prejudice them at the moment we are trying to put our lives in order. But this is not an end in itself...But our man is sure to be impressed with a sincere desire to set right the wrong. He is going to be more

interested in a demonstration of good will than in our talk of spiritual discoveries." – Big Book, pgs. 76-77.

For some people who we may have hurt or wronged in our addictions, they may not be open to hearing about this new life we have or are living. It is not about the words that we are saying but the actions that we are doing. And this should make sense for some of us. How many times have we told people the word "sorry" and said that we are "going to change" before falling right back into our same patterns of destruction? In recovery, life must become less about words and more about action. Therefore, saying you are living a spiritual life or one of philosophy (if you ask me, they are very similar) does not mean as much as showing everyone what living that life means and looks like.

Going back to my example. I can tell you that the last part is quite true. People who had wondered or had issues with me studying philosophy have seen the change in my life and how I am on any day. My partner recently told me how much she has seen the change that has taken place in my life and admires the person I am becoming. The family member who was afraid I was going to worship Zeus has commented that she does not care what I am reading; all she cares about is the positive change and growth I have shown since following it. I get asked to be a speaker at meetings more often about the crazy story I have about my addictions and the change I showed, and how I had gotten to it. Some people might still mock, but those voices become fewer and fewer (besides, a part of Stoicism is not caring about what others say). People will see the changes in you as you study this philosophy. It becomes undeniable, and the admiration comes from the fact that your chosen philosophy is solely focused on becoming a good person.

The final warning from Epictetus is about staying dedicated to it. If you give in to the naysayers and stop studying philosophy, there is the chance that they might even mock you or make fun of you even more (double ridicule). Because not only were they already making fun of you for studying philosophy, but then you gave up, so they were obviously right (in their own eyes).

Remember that this is about you becoming a better you.

Stick to it.

"You just have to prove to yourself that you can go out there and be the best that you can be and not prove anything to anyone." – *Serena Williams*

CHAPTER 23

Be Content With Yourself
(Courage, Temperance)

If you ever happen to turn your attention to externals, for the pleasure of anyone, be assured that you have ruined your scheme of life. Be content, then, in everything, with being a philosopher; and if you wish to seem so likewise to anyone, appear so to yourself, and it will suffice you. – Chapter 23, Epictetus' Enchiridion.

I f someone wants you to value all those other things in life that are outside of the person you are, then your plan will be ruined. If they want you to be more concerned about money, property, and possessions rather than being a virtuous person, then you will be in danger of journeying down a dark road. And as you live the life of a Stoic, this could be a scenario you will have to face. We can often find the world to be a materialistic place. Many people see what you have (externals) rather than who you are as being something more important.

This can be a dangerous road for us in recovery. Sometimes, after having a bit of sobriety under our belts, we can shift our focus from our recovery to getting back all those things we might have lost in our addictions. We can see life becoming once again about getting the job we need, the nice place to live, the nice car, and all those possessions we might have lost. This loss of focus on our recovery and becoming better can lead us to failure and relapse. It may not be a part of your story, but I have heard from many people that it was a part of theirs. And it was a part of my own. Getting back those external things in life became more important than my recovery and character growth. This led me to a relapse and a bottom even worse than any experienced before.

Losing focus would cause catastrophic destruction.

It may not even be your own doing that causes this lack of focus. One common piece of advice is to avoid relationships in the first year of recovery so that you can focus on yourself rather than turn your attention to another person's wants and needs. Because unfortunately, sometimes, the people we choose to bring into our lives can shift our focus from what we value to other things. And this is what Epictetus is warning about in this passage. If someone comes into your life and has you turning your attention to all those external things that Stoicism says we need to learn not to value as much, then there is a good chance that your Stoic plan will be ruined.

Seeking outside validation is something common that many people suffer from. It is thought that this could come from the fact that when we begin our lives, we entirely depend on others as children, and something along the way can damage this so that we continue to desire this even in adulthood (Cikanavicius 2017). Most of the stories I have heard in the rooms of recovery have had a damaged childhood associated with them, which could be why codependency and seeking outside validation are common characteristics of addicts.

The only person who you need validation from is yourself. Do not let anyone else compromise your goals or alter your path to a virtuous life. Do not let anyone turn you away from focusing your attention on yourself and place it on external things that do not matter in the bigger picture of life. If they have an issue with that, then maybe they are not a good person to have in your life, and it is an unhealthy relationship you have with them in whatever form it may be.

I think this is critical to those of us in recovery. During our addictions, things can get so bad that we could possibly truly hate who we are and what we are doing. We hate who we have become, which can even lead to suicidal thoughts. Therefore, in recovery, we need to find that loving ourselves and who we are is the most important thing that we need. As Epictetus says at the end of this, dedicate your life to philosophy (becoming a person of excellent character). If you need anyone to like yourself, you be that person, and in the end, you will find that this is all you need.

Be who you want to be.

Not what others wish for you.

The only approval you need is that of yourself.

"When you say yes to others, make sure you aren't saying no to yourself." – Paulo Coehlo

CHAPTER 24

You Are Somebody
(Justice, Wisdom)

Let not such considerations as these distress you: "I shall live in discredit and be nobody anywhere." For if discredit be an evil, you can no more be involved in evil through another than in baseness. Is it any business of yours, then, to get power or to be admitted to an entertainment? By no means. How then, after all, is this discredit? And how it is true that you will be nobody anywhere when you ought to be somebody in those things only which are within your own power, in which you may be of the greatest consequence? – Chapter 24, Epictetus' Enchiridion.

How many followers do I have? How many likes did my post get? How many dislikes? What kind of comments? How many people shared it?

Social media is a business that thrives on the human desire to feel accepted and known. Studies have found that social media can trigger the brain's reward systems (like other addictions...which is why we must be careful with using it). It also feeds on the desire to be accepted by society and seen by the world (King University 2019). It is as if there is this common trait among humanity (addict or not) that what we do or what we have does not have a value until other people have given their approval. And research is already finding among teens that fewer likes on their posts can lead to higher levels of depression and anxiety along with lower values of self-worth (Reshanov 2020).

In this chapter, Epictetus revisits the concept of seeking validation from external sources, a topic previously discussed. This time, he probes deeper into the human desire for reputation and recognition, emphasizing our inherent need for validation from others. The fear of being overlooked or considered insignificant—of being a 'nobody'—is an age-old concern that even resonates with contemporary issues like social media, despite thousands of years preceding its existence.

Those of us who have suffered from addiction may have felt this fear of being unrecognized in our own ways as well. I vividly recall feeling like a mere speck in the world during the depths of my addiction—utterly lost and insignificant. The idea of disappearing or even dying seemed inconsequential, as I believed nobody would miss me or even notice my absence. And from various meetings I have attended and conversations with other addicts, I have discovered that I was not alone in having this feeling.

Epictetus challenges the idea that being unrecognized or living in discredit is a genuine problem. He questions whether it truly matters to us to gain power or be accepted at social events. The answer is that it should not be our business to seek these external validations. Instead, he encourages us to focus on what is genuinely within our control. Remember that our reputation is not within our control and is a power that belongs to others. The number of followers you have, the likes you get, the comments you receive, and the shares on your posts are out of your power and belong in the hands of others. So being unknown cannot be evil because the opposite (being known) belongs to other people.

He then points out that it is unrealistic to say that you can be a nobody everywhere in your life because you can be somebody in everything you control. He reminds us that we should only seek to be somebody in those areas where we have agency, those things within our own power. This includes our character, actions, decisions, and how we respond to events. You interact with people every day of your life in all the different activities that you do. You have so many roles that are given to you to play (remember life as a stage), and it is entirely in your control to excel in these aspects of your life. And to the people you affect every day of your life, you will be somebody. Maybe the entire world does not know your name or your existence, but if you are making the most of your life, you will be known to the people (family, friends, etc.) who matter the most.

I feel that this is the part that those suffering from addiction must focus on most. We may think that we are unknown and can die or disappear without being noticed, but this is far from the truth. One of the hardest parts of staying in sober living for a few years is that you eventually deal with the deaths of others at the hands of addiction. And the one thing I quickly learned at all the memorials I had attended is that every single one of those who died was somebody to multiple people.

"But my friends will be unassisted." What do you mean by "unassisted"? They will not have money from you, nor will you make them Roman citizens. Who told you, then, that these are among the

things within our own power, and not rather the affairs of others? And who can give to another the things which he himself has not? "Well, but get them, then, that we too may have a share." If I can get them with the preservation of my own honor and fidelity and self-respect, show me the way and I will get them; but if you require me to lose my own proper good, that you may gain what is no good, consider how unreasonable and foolish you are. Besides, which would you rather have, a sum of money or a faithful and honorable friend? Rather assist me, then, to gain this character than require me to do those things by which I may lose it. – Chapter 24, Epictetus' Enchiridion

———————

Is it right to do something wrong to help the people you care for in your life? The people that you are somebody to? This is an often-discussed philosophical question: "do the ends justify the means?" If we get something good in the end, does it matter what wrong things we had to do along the way (the means)?

Some of us, in our addictions, lived out a twisted version of this concept. We would lie, cheat, or steal (the means) to feed our addictions (the ends). Of course, we knew that what we were doing was wrong, but if it got us to feed our addictions, we were totally fine in doing it. In fact, these actions could be the cause for some of the amends that we have to make to others in our recovery. But the worst part of it all was not only were the means wrong we were doing, but the ends that we were aiming for were not even good as well.

So now you are in recovery. Is it okay to continue to do bad things (lie, cheat and steal) if the ends you are aiming for are no longer selfish but are now trying to help others who are important in your life?

Of course not.

Epictetus first reminds us that the lives of others are not in our control. When another person needs something, it is ultimately up to them to get it for themselves. And that we cannot give to another person things that we do not already have in our own possession. So, does this mean we never help other people?

"For as these were made to perform a particular function, and, by performing it according to their own constitution, gain in full what is due to them, so likewise, a human being is formed by nature to benefit others, and, when he has performed some benevolent action or accomplished anything else that contributes to the common good, he has done what he was constituted for, and has what is properly his." – Marcus Aurelius, Meditations, 9:42.

As discussed throughout this book, justice is one of the four Stoic virtues. And as Marcus Aurelius discusses above, doing things for others is one of the main reasons we exist. It is why we are alive on this planet and a part of humanity. Therefore, we should be actively looking for ways in which we should try to benefit people who are in our life. However, it all depends on the help you are being asked to give and how you do it. If you can be someone who helps another while maintaining your virtuous character, help. It is almost your duty to help. But if you must abandon the person you aim to be to help, then you cannot do it. In Stoicism, the means become more important than the ends. It no longer matters about what we are getting out of something but how we do it.

If someone pushes you into trying to do something wrong to get something good, you need to reevaluate that friendship or relationship with the person. Epictetus perfectly discusses this when he asks, would these people in your life rather have money or a faithful and honorable friend? The people in our lives should find it more critical to help us grow and cultivate our moral character rather than asking of us things that will destroy it.

Once, we might have lived a life where what we did was of no concern if we got what we needed. Now we must live a life where what we do is the essential thing in the actions we commit and not as much the results. During our addictions, we might have surrounded ourselves with people who lived by those same old standards we used to. Now in our recovery, we must question those relationships to see if they will be supportive of our new ways and the new person we want and need to be.

———————

Well, but my country, say you, as far as depends upon me, will be unassisted. Here, again, what assistance is this you mean? It will not have porticos nor baths of your providing? And what signifies that? Why, neither does a smith provide it with shoes, nor a shoemaker with arms. It is enough if everyone fully performs his own proper business. And were you to supply it with another faithful and honorable citizen, would not he be of use to it? Yes. Therefore neither are you yourself useless to it. "What place, then," say you, "shall I hold in the state?" Whatever you can hold with the preservation of your fidelity and honor. But if, by desiring to be useful to that, you lose these, how can you serve your country when you have become faithless and shameless? – Chapter 24, Epictetus' Enchiridion.

———————

"Ask not what your country can do for you, ask what you can do for your country." – John F. Kennedy

People feel a sense of pride and honor for the country in which they were born (or may have immigrated to). I think of the Olympic opening ceremonies, where athletes who have dedicated their lives to their sport march proudly into the stadium behind their country's flag, wearing the chosen uniform for that year. Some athletes playing the sport professionally in other countries might even return to one of their birth to represent it in the games. The Olympics is a massive event in which these individuals from countries worldwide gather in one location to show what they will do for their country.

However, the Olympics are not free from controversy. You can easily search online for many examples of athletes finding various ways to cheat to gain an advantage in their competition performance. Sometimes the athletes make these choices themselves. Sometimes it is their own country that asks them to do it. In relation to the previous section, they use corrupted means to achieve the desired end.

In the previous part, Epictetus discussed how wrongful acts to help someone in our lives are not something we can be a part of. But is it okay if we do these things to help our country? After all, we are doing this not for just one person but for the greater good of many.

The simple answer...

No.

"I am not an Athenian or a Greek, but a citizen of the world."
– Socrates

There is nothing wrong with having pride and honor for the country that you are from. But Stoic justice is not something that the lines of the country will bind. We may feel a closer kinship with people from the same place we are from, but all of humanity, no matter what country they are from, are related. Just because someone lives in a country that is not your own does not mean they are undeserving of your virtuous actions. We need to take all of humanity into account in the things that we do. Therefore, even if it is something that your country is asking for you to do, we still must look at it through the virtuous Stoic lenses. We need to make sure we are not sacrificing our character.

So, what can we give to our country?

Epictetus discusses that what every country truly needs are citizens that are loyal and honorable. This is something everyone can give to it. This is something that you can give to it.

Right now.

Today.

Some of us might have had run-ins with the law (I know I did) in our addictions, and we were not giving our country the citizens it needs to succeed. When you are breaking the law, you are literally doing what your country asks you not to do. So, in our recovery, the one thing our country needs the most from us is for us to follow the law and not make things worse.

This does not mean you cannot do more for your country. For example, you can be a police officer (if your past record does not get in the way). Join the military. Organize movements for issues that concern you (no country is perfect). Attend protests. You can even run for political office (Seneca was the advisor to the emperor, and Marcus Aurelius was an emperor). But, no matter what you choose, you must do it in a way that maintains your honor and loyalty (you cannot be a shady politician) so that you keep the virtuous person that you are. Because if you must compromise these in trying to do your part, you become more useless than useful.

Almost everyone needs to feel recognized or noticed. We want to feel like we are somebody to people rather than a complete nobody. And everyone can do this. We have people in our lives that we interact with every day. We have a country we live in and fellow citizens with whom we share it. So, we can affect our country and the people who are in our lives. But we need to make sure that in all our actions, we consider our goal to be the best person we can be.

Whether for your country…

Or another person…

The end is not as important…

Since actions matter more.

"To the world, you may be one person; but to one person you may be the world." – Dr. Suess

No Reason to Be Jealous
(Justice, Temperance)

Is anyone preferred before you at an entertainment, or in courtesies, or in confidential intercourse? If these things are good, you ought to rejoice that he has them; and if they are evil, do not be grieved that you have them not. And remember that you cannot be permitted to rival others in externals without using the same means to obtain them. For how can he who will not haunt the door of any man, will not attend him, will not praise him, have an equal share with him who does these things? You are unjust, then, and unreasonable if you are unwilling to pay the price for which these things are sold, and would have them for nothing.
– Chapter 25, Epictetus' Enchiridion.

———————

Did someone get invited to a party, gathering, or event rather than you? Did someone get a compliment that you felt you deserved as well? Or were they asked for advice you thought you would have been better at giving?

Returning once again to the idea of reputation and the fact that we have no control over the choices or actions of others, Epictetus focuses a bit more on the importance of learning to let go and not be concerned with such things. Because we can often discover the roots of jealousy in seeing others having a reputation or an opportunity to do something we feel should have been given to us. And the jealousy issue is that it is not only a lousy emotion in and of itself, but it can also lead to resentment in the long run if we do not do something about it. And everyone in recovery knows the dangers of resentment and what it can mean for our continued sobriety.

"It is plain that a life which includes deep resentment leads only to futility and unhappiness...this business of resentment is infinitely grave. We found that it is fatal. For when harboring such feelings we shut ourselves off from the sunlight of the Spirit." – Big Book, Page 66.

Epictetus focuses this first part of the chapter on three different scenarios:

1. If someone rightfully gets something good.
2. If someone gets something that is not good.
3. If someone gets something good, but it has a cost to it.

You find yourself in a situation in which someone is given something that you might want (invitation, compliment, asked for advice, etc.). And now you find the claws of jealousy scratching deeply within your mind and gut. It would be best if you took a moment to analyze the situation, think of which of these three categories it falls under, and then act accordingly.

Just as I have discussed throughout this book, it is essential to embrace the notion that we are all interconnected on this planet, and we should see others not as adversaries but as part of a collective whole. Consequently, when someone receives something good or experiences success, we should rejoice for them and avoid jealousy. In fact, when something good happens to another person, we can view it as something positive happening to humanity as a whole, strengthening the bond that connects us all. Celebrating others' achievements reinforces a sense of community and shared joy.

Conversely, when something negative or undesirable is offered or requested, it should not trouble us. Not everything that people receive or seek is beneficial or appealing to us. Just as an alcoholic may not care about being invited to a bar night out, we all have preferences and boundaries regarding compliments, advice, or invitations.

What about those people who get the good things but get them through questionable ways? Relating to the last chapter, their means to get to those ends were dubious. Epictetus presents this situation next and throughout the rest of the chapter in a "sell your soul to the devil" manner. Sometimes people will get something you may have wanted but had to do something to receive it.

When someone has something we want for ourselves, we are under their control to get it. So, what will the price be? You might have to always be there when they need something from you (haunt the door), attend to them (do what they ask), or praise or flatter them with words you do not mean. This is the selling of the soul. Are you willing to do whatever this person asks of you so that you can get what you want in return? Epictetus points out that you are a person who is unjust and unreasonable if you want something that someone possesses but are unwilling to pay the price for it.

———

For how much is lettuce sold? Fifty cents, for instance. If another, then, paying fifty cents, takes the lettuce, and you, not paying it, go without them, don't imagine that he has gained any advantage over you. For as he has the lettuce, so you have the fifty cents which you did not give. So, in the present case, you have not been invited to such a person's entertainment, because you have not paid him the price for which a supper is sold. It is sold for praise; it is sold for attendance. Give him then the value, if it is for your advantage. But if you would, at the same time, not pay the one and yet receive the other, you are insatiable, and a blockhead. Have you nothing, then, instead of the supper? Yes, indeed, you have: the not praising him, whom you don't like to praise; the not bearing with his behavior at coming in. – Chapter 25, Epictetus' Enchiridion.

———

But is it always so bad not to get something we want?

Epictetus further expands on this concept of selling your soul to complete this chapter. He begins with the simple idea of buying lettuce. He discusses a situation where one person will pay the price for a head of lettuce (fifty cents in this example), and you are unwilling to. First, you cannot expect to get any lettuce because you were not willing to pay for it. But just because the person has lettuce does not make them better than you because you still have the fifty cents that you chose not to spend.

He then uses this example to explain the price further to get something from another person. For example, you were not invited to an event that someone was throwing because the cost of going to it would involve having to flatter them (kiss their ass) or do something they want you to do. If it is important for you to go and it will benefit you, do it. But if you are not willing to do those things required to get invited, then you would be an idiot to expect to be.

But much like the lettuce, you are not empty-handed.

Yes, you did not get invited. But what did you get out of it? Well, you did not have to do those things that this person may have required of others to get the invite. For example, you did not have to praise and flatter them with words that you did not believe in. And you did not have to be around someone who would expect such things from other people. In other words, you were able to hold on to your pride.

In the end, if you discover that you have jealousy over something that someone may have obtained from another person that you had felt you deserved, take a moment and a breath (as so often recommended). Before allowing this to grow into resentment over the giver or receiver, ask yourself which of these three situations it is.

1. Was it something good that the person truly deserved?
2. Was it something bad or evil that you should not really want?
3. Was it something that had a cost associated with it you were unwilling to pay?

Answering which of these three categories it falls under will give you peace of mind and a release from jealousy.

"The envious die not once, but as oft as the envied win applause."
– Baltasar Gracian

CHAPTER 26

Listen to Your Own Advice
(Justice, Wisdom)

The will of nature may be learned from things upon which we are all agreed. As when our neighbor's boy has broken a cup, or the like, we are ready at once to say, "These are casualties that will happen"; be assured, then, that when your own cup is likewise broken, you ought to be affected just as when another's cup was broken. Now apply this to greater things. Is the child or wife of another dead? There is no one who would not say, "This is an accident of mortality." But if anyone's own child happens to die, it is immediately, "Alas! how wretched am I!" It should be always remembered how we are affected on hearing the same thing concerning others. – Chapter 26, Epictetus' Enchiridion.

When bad things happen in life, do not be a hypocrite! Once again, Epictetus suggests another route or way to deal with the unfortunate events that happen to us in life to avoid the negative emotions that such occurrences create. And I guess the easiest way to sum up what he is saying here is that when something terrible happens to someone, remember what you said to them when it happens to you. Then use those exact words that you gave to them on yourself.

When something breaks for someone, we can easily tell them such things as: "you got a lot of use out of it," "you can always get a new one," or maybe even "you can get a better one now." We might even say to them, "shit happens" (these are casualties that will happen). Think of what we say when car accidents happen to others, words like: "it could have been worse," "luckily you are still alive," or "it will get fixed." And if we see someone overreacting, we might even wonder why the person is acting that way.

It is funny how people can think so level-minded and clear-headed about the accidents and unfortunate events that happen to other people. Having that separation from the event by it not occurring to us allows for us to look at it from a rational perspective. But as soon as the same thing happens to us, that level-headedness is right out the window, and now it is a tragic event. Think about this for a second. It is the same thing that has happened to you that you have witnessed countless times with others. Why should it be any different or more special now that you must deal with it?

Epictetus points out that we need to even think of the things we say to others when greater tragedies, like death, occur to someone. We might say something like: "they lived a good life," "they lived a long life," or even "they are in a better place now." We find ways to comfort other people with words even when they have to deal with the death of a loved one, and we can see the event with a rational mind state somehow. Yet, when death happens to someone close to us these words become absent in our thoughts.

As discussed earlier in this book, playing the victim is something that so many of us in addiction are so good at doing. But in our recovery, we need to stop taking on this role because it could be a potential trigger for our relapse. The more we feel wronged by an event that has occurred, the closer we step towards possibly using our drug of choice to ease and comfort those negative emotions that have been stirred up.

When bad things happen to you in life, remember how you see those same events when they happen to another person. Remember the level-headedness that you can examine and look at the situation with. Remember the advice you can give them to get through it. It is unjust and bad character to think that because this has happened to you, it differs from when it happened to another person.

Therefore, you have the best advice and path to get through any tragedy or unfortunate event you may encounter. That advice (if you were sincere in your words) is the same advice you tell others. So, when such things occur, recall the mind-state that you applied for other people, the words you used, and now use those exact words on yourself.

"Sometimes the advice you tell other people, is the advice that you need to follow." – Author unknown

CHAPTER 27

Evil Is Within
(Wisdom)

As a mark is not set up for the sake of missing the aim, so neither does the nature of evil exist in the world. – Chapter 27, Epictetus' Enchiridion.

The world is not against you.

The simple line that comprises this entire chapter is something that many of us who have dealt with addiction need to remember daily throughout our lives. As discussed multiple times throughout this book, those who have suffered from addiction can often develop this mind state of being the victim. We can sometimes feel we were dealt an unfair hand in life compared to other people around us. And we sometimes can use this feeling to justify why we are addicts. Because the world has been unfair, I need to use my drug of choice to handle it.

But we need to think of the big picture.

Is it really logical to think that God came along and out of the billions of people on the planet, chose you to be the brunt of evil?

Selected your life solely as the one for all bad things to happen to. And if you do not believe in God, is it logical to think that merely Nature and the universe itself somehow had this ability to select you as the one that all bad things will happen to?

Epictetus discusses in this chapter that the world is not set up for things to go badly. It is not designed specifically for us to miss the mark we aim for. It is not aiming for our failure.

During our addictions, it might feel as if the world is against us. As if life was just not being fair. We may even have wondered why we had to deal with things that we do not see others dealing with. But we never really stopped to notice that it was not that the world was against us; we were living in misery because of the self-inflicted punishment that we were delivering to ourselves. Bad things happened because we caused them to happen. Therefore, life can seem to go so much better for us in recovery because we have finally stopped doing the one main thing that was the root cause of our misery.

Now I know that some of you may think or wonder why "bad" (evil) things happen in this world. But you have to ask yourself if it is merely God or the universe causing those things to occur to you or are they the actions of others or simply chance events (even natural disasters have specific things that cause them).

> "The point is that nobody errs on purpose. Whatever we do, we think it is the right thing to do, according to whatever criterion we have developed or adopted to establish right action…evil is often the result of lack of thought, meaning that people don't want to do evil, and certainly don't think of themselves as evil doers. But they also tend to follow the general opinion without critical analysis…." – Massimo Pigliucci, How to Be a Stoic, pgs. 111-112.

A rather enlightening aspect of Stoicism that I discovered is their view on the nature of evil. It has allowed me to see the actions of others from a healthier perspective. To the Stoics, evil comes from within us and not the world. Once we have learned about the right way to live (a virtuous one), we commit evil acts when we choose not to live that way.

I know this might seem to contradict how you may have lived to this point. We can easily think of things such as murder and rape as acts of evil that others commit. But the Stoics view that people only do things they consider beneficial to themselves. So, nobody would do anything they see as harmful to themselves. Murderers and rapists will easily provide reasons they felt the need to commit those acts from a view that they had seen as beneficial to themselves. What we would see as being acts of evil by others actually have origins within a skewed mental perspective. It should be something pitied more than anything. It is a further example of how we need to hold back our desire to cast judgments on things around us, especially when it involves events beyond our control (such as acts committed by others).

You can find this view even discussed in the Bible when Jesus was crucified on the cross; he said:

"Father, forgive them, for they do not know what they are doing."
– Luke, 23:34.

In the moment that Jesus was being crucified on the cross at the hands of other humans, he knew that it was because of their flawed perspective that the action was occurring and his own life was being taken away. But rather than having anger, he chose acceptance and compassion for the people over this wrongful deed. We need to begin to see what we would have viewed as the misdeeds from others from a similar perspective. We have to see their own humanity and confusions in knowing what is right or wrong.

Think of how some of us may have acted amid our addictions. We may have done wrong things to get our drug of choice. But would we have thought of ourselves as evil people? I know I did not. I just had a skewed view of what was more important in life. Continuing my habit was more important than anything else. So, I would willingly commit wrongful acts (lying, cheating, and stealing) to maintain my addictions.

Now I am living a life of recovery. I know it is wrong to lie, cheat, and steal to feed addictive behaviors. And now, I choose to live the life of a Stoic, which means that my purpose is to live a virtuous existence. Anything I do that contradicts my life of Stoicism and recovery is evil or bad acts I commit since I know I should not be doing them. I can no longer make excuses for it.

Therefore, the only source of evil is from within us. But as for the world, specifically selecting us to be the one person to whom all bad things happen is not the reality. So be wise in the choices you make. Remember the ignorance of others in the choices that they make. And keep your aim on that mark of living a life of excellence.

"There is an evil in all of us, and it is the mark of a man how he defies the evil within." – David Gemmell

CHAPTER 28

Own Your Mind
(Temperance)

If a person had delivered up your body to some passer-by, you would certainly be angry. And do you feel no shame in delivering up your own mind to any reviler, to be disconcerted and confounded? – Chapter 28, Epictetus' Enchiridion.

This simple passage is another reminder of what happens when we allow someone else to cause negative emotions (anger, jealousy, resentment, etc.) inside of us. I like it because it gives a bigger-picture perspective on what is occurring in the situation. Suppose someone was to come along and tell you that your physical body belongs to them or someone else; there is probably a good chance that you would be pretty angry or bothered by that. You would probably do whatever you had within your power to gain back control of your physical body and keep it in your possession.

So why would you allow someone to do that with your mind?

Think of what happens when someone says something that angers you. You often get stuck thinking about that person and what they have said. You think less about what you are doing and all that is happening around you while focusing more on them. Sometimes, an entire day of your existence can be ruined merely because this person said something you disapproved of.

That person owns your mind.

They own your thoughts.

They even control your emotions.

The worst part about all of this is that you have a person that has done something that you do not agree with. Yet, in the process of all of this, you are now freely giving this person part of your being. Someone that you are bothered by owns your most valuable asset.

> "...yet when it comes to the matter of wasting time, in the case of the one thing in which it is right to be miserly, they show themselves the most prodigal (wrecklessly spending)...though all the while that day which you bestow on some person or thing is perhaps your last." – Seneca, On the Shortness of Life, Chapter III.

The issue is that not only are you giving this person your mind and allowing them to give you negative emotions, but you are also giving them your time, the most precious resource you have in your existence. And what would happen if this was your last day to live (it possibly could be)? Would you like to know that you spent it with your thoughts in the grasp of another person?

Only you can set yourself free.

Therefore, do not let the words that someone has said take control of your mind. Do not give them the satisfaction of possessing the one thing that truly belongs to you while stealing your most precious resource (time). You should be bothered that you are letting them own your mind, anyway. It is in your grasp and control to set yourself free. Live and let go. In doing so, they lose ownership, and you regain it.

"Control your own mind, and you may never be controlled by the mind of another." – Napoleon Hill

CHAPTER 29

Know What It Will Take
(Courage, Wisdom)

In every affair consider what precedes and what follows, and then undertake it. Otherwise, you will begin with spirit, indeed, careless of the consequences, and when these are developed, you will shamefully desist. "I would conquer at the Olympic Games." But consider what precedes and what follows, and then, if it be for your advantage, engage in the affair. You must conform to rules, submit to a diet, refrain from dainties; exercise your body, whether you choose it or not, at a stated hour, in heat and cold; you must drink no cold water, and sometimes no wine—in a word, you must give yourself up to your trainer as to a physician. Then, in the combat, you may be thrown into a ditch, dislocate your arm, turn your ankle, swallow an abundance of dust, receive stripes [for negligence], and, after all, lose the victory. When you have reckoned up all this, if your inclination still holds, set about the combat. – Chapter 29, Epictetus' Enchiridion.

P retty much everyone has goals they want to accomplish in life. For those in recovery, maintaining our sobriety is one of them. But there can be different goals beyond this:

- Getting a house or a car.
- Getting into a new relationship.
- Repairing the relationships we may have destroyed.

For me and some people I have met in recovery, the path to a new career became one.

In any goal or project you commit toward, you need to consider what it will take to begin and what to expect. Without doing this, there is a chance that the excitement you begin with disappears when difficulties arise, leading you to quit. Therefore, think about what it will take to achieve a goal, and if you are ready for it, then make it your endeavor.

Epictetus uses the example of an athlete (Olympian) to illustrate his point. To be an athlete, you have to eat the proper diet and stay away from sweets (dainties), exercise your body even if you do not feel like it at the time you are supposed to, no matter what the weather is, and give yourself over to the power of your trainer as if he was your doctor. Before you choose the path of an athlete, these are things you should expect your life to be about to reach your goal. And despite all the work you put into becoming this athlete, you might still lose. As the Stoics constantly remind us throughout their work, we can aim for a goal, but whether or not we hit the target is outside our control. And at the end of thinking about these considerations, if it still seems worth it to train as an athlete, then do it; if it does not, then search for another goal.

If sobriety is your goal, what will it take for you to maintain it other than simply not partaking in your drug of choice? Will it require weekly meetings or daily ones? Will it require a sponsor or a mentor? Will it require sessions with a therapist? What will you do when the difficult times in life that can threaten your sobriety occur?

So often, we can fail to maintain our sobriety because we lose sight of what we need to do to maintain it. We become that Olympic athlete who gives up on the necessary parts of training only to find out we were nowhere near prepared for the games. I know that many times I attempted to get sober were made without thinking of the life changes I would have to commit to simply beyond no drinking or doing drugs. As a result, I would always find myself in relapse, wondering what I did wrong while not realizing I was only putting in half-hearted attempts.

Another example to consider in recovery is rebuilding relationships that we might have destroyed throughout our addictions. What will it take for you to do that? How will you have to reach out to them? What amends could you expect to have to make? Are you willing to understand that it could take years to rebuild them? And with all these questions answered, knowing all that you might have to do, will it still be worth it to you knowing there is still a chance that it may never happen?

"The mind adapts and turns around any obstacle to action to serve its objectives; a hindrance to a given work is turned to its furtherance, an obstacle in a given path becomes an advance." – *Marcus Aurelius, Meditations, 5:20.*

In this Stoic quote, we can again see the idea of changing your perspective on how you see things in life. For the difficulties that you can see in reaching your goal, or as new ones come along the way, you are given a clear picture of what you need to do to continue. As the modern Stoic Ryan Holiday said, this is called "the obstacle is the way." It is the difficulties we encounter that give us clear guidance on what we need to do or overcome to reach a goal. A rock in the road of progress gives us insight into what we need to overcome to keep progressing. I have applied it by thinking, well, at least I am not lost and know what I need to do to keep moving forward.

What goals do you have right now? What will it take for you to begin your progress toward these goals? What difficulties can you expect along the way? And what will you do if you fail at first? Answer these questions before any project you take on in life, and you should find yourself ready to face difficulties and give yourself a better chance at achieving success in the end. But always remember that there is a chance that you may never reach that goal (the athlete who might still lose in the end).

Otherwise, take notice, you will behave like children who sometimes play wrestlers, sometimes gladiators, sometimes blow a trumpet, and sometimes act a tragedy, when they happen to have seen and admired these shows. Thus you too will be at one time a wrestler, and another a gladiator; now a philosopher, now an orator; but nothing in earnest. Like an ape you mimic all you see, and one thing after another is sure to please you, but is out of favor as soon as it becomes familiar. For you have never entered upon anything considerately; nor after having surveyed and tested the whole matter, but carelessly, and with a halfway zeal. – Chapter 29, Epictetus' Enchiridion.

Have you ever known someone (or it could be you) that is constantly changing their plans in life? For a while, they have one goal, then change it up to another, then change into another, then another, and again and again and again. Finally, they never reach the end and achieve anything they had set out to do since they never put all their focus into one. In the passage above, Epictetus likens this to children who constantly change different roles or characters they imagine themselves to be as they play every day. He also compares this to apes that mimic what they see someone doing and then move on to something else when they grow tired of it.

If we continually change our goals and constantly shift them to other things, then it keeps us from putting all of ourselves into the main goal that we are focused on at that time, moving on to something else when we grow tired of it, or if difficulties get in the way. If we genuinely looked deeply into the project or goal we have chosen and looked at what it would take to achieve it and asked ourselves if it were worth it, then there would be less of a chance of us constantly shifting what we want to achieve. Of course, it is okay to start something out and find out that it may not be for you in the middle of it. However, if this is becoming a typical pattern, then you need to ask yourself if you are genuinely thinking deeply about if this is what you want and will accept what it takes to get there before you begin.

"It is not that we have a short space of time, but that we waste much of it. Life is long enough, and it has been given in sufficiently generous measure to allow the accomplishment of the very greatest things if the whole of it is well invested. But when it is squandered in luxury and carelessness, when it is devoted to no good end, forced at last by the ultimate necessity we perceive that it has

passed away before we were aware that it was passing. So it is— the life we receive is not short, but we make it so, nor do we have any lack of it, but are wasteful of it." – Seneca, On the Shortness of Life, Chapter I.

We often hear people saying that "life is too short." The Stoic quote above is one of my favorites and one that I have often thought about. The idea that life is too short only happens because we make it that way. We have so much time to accomplish many things, but we are wasteful and careless with that time. At the end of our life, it seems as if it was too short to get what we wanted to accomplish because we just threw away the time allotted. However, life is perfectly long enough if we learn to use the time we are given wisely.

This is the ultimate warning that Epictetus was giving. If we do not wisely choose the goals and projects we take in life, making ourselves aware of what it will take to achieve them and if it will be worth it. If we do not dedicate our hearts and souls to the endeavors that we choose. We could easily find ourselves jumping around from one thing to another and never completing anything we set out to do. And when we come to the end of our life, we will feel as if it was too short, and we never got to do anything we had wanted to do, not realizing that we had been careless with our time and our efforts in a self-sabotaging way.

———

Thus some, when they have seen a philosopher and heard a man speaking like Euphrates—though, indeed, who can speak like him?— have a mind to be philosophers, too. Consider first, man, what the matter is, and what your own nature is able to bear. If you would be a wrestler, consider your shoulders, your back, your thighs; for different persons are made for different things. Do you think that you can act as you do and be a philosopher, that you can eat, drink, be angry, be discontented, as you are now? You must watch, you must labor, you must get the better of certain appetites, must quit your acquaintances, be despised by your servant, be laughed at by those you meet; come off worse than others in everything—in offices, in honors, before tribunals. When you have fully considered all these things, approach, if you please—that is, if, by parting with them, you have a mind to purchase serenity, freedom, and tranquility. If not, do not come hither; do not, like children, be now a philosopher, then a publican, then an orator, and then one of Caesar's officers. These things are not consistent. You must be one man, either good or bad. You must cultivate either your own reason or else externals; apply yourself either to things within or without you—that is, be either a philosopher or one of the mob. – Chapter 29, Epictetus' Enchiridion.

The last part of this chapter gets to the ultimate goal that Epictetus was aiming for. Do you have what it takes to live this life of philosophy (Stoicism)? Do you understand what it will require and what it will take to continue to live it? We are often told that the road to recovery is not easy. Similarly, Epictetus is saying that living a philosopher's life is not easy either (which is why I think recovery and philosophy go hand in hand with each other).

The thing to understand is that when he speaks of being a philosopher, it differs from what many of us think of it in modern times. When people think of a philosopher, they conjure up this image of a person writing books or leading discussions on the subject.

However, much like how an athlete is not creating a sport, just following the rules of one, the philosopher is a person who adheres to a philosophy and lives the life it describes.

But do you understand what you will have to do?

"Philosophy is an art of living that cures us of our illnesses by teaching a radically new way of life." – Arnold Davidson, Philosophy as a Way of Life, pg. 28.

To live as a philosopher is to see the cure for illnesses (such as addiction) as a radically new way of living. You may have to change some of your old habits, such as what you eat or drink (Stoics discussed the dangers of alcoholism), and work on anger issues and dissatisfaction in life. You need to stay present in the moment (to no longer waste time), work hard to gain control and conquer those desires that negatively impact you. There might be certain friends you cannot be around any longer (we should realize this early in our recovery), and as stated in an earlier chapter, people may mock you for being a philosopher. You have to be willing to let go and let others get the better of situations as you give up thoughts of revenge and cling to those external things outside of your control. But the main point is understanding what it will take to live this way.

So why would it be worth it?

Because of what it gives.

Control over your emotions, freedom, and tranquility.

Stoics believe in progress over perfection and know it will take time and work to get better at the practice. And to do this, you must stay steady on your chosen path. You cannot be focused on growing mentally and a person of excellent character one day, then obsessed with worldly things and the external the next. It's not possible to hop back and forth like children. Put your heart and soul into one. Of course, you can choose the way of the world, which is most likely how you have lived for most of your life, or the road less traveled, as Robert Frost had said in his poem. But the point is that you cannot do both.

The choice is yours.

The life of a philosopher…or being like everyone else.

Just know what will be required.

"Decide whether or not the goal is worth the risks involved. If it is, stop worrying." – Amelia Earhart

CHAPTER 30

Do Your Duty
(Justice)

Duties are universally measured by relations. Is a certain man your father? In this are implied taking care of him, submitting to him in all things, patiently receiving his reproaches, his correction. But he is a bad father. Is your natural tie, then, to a good father? No, but to a father. Is a brother unjust? Well, preserve your own just relation toward him. Consider not what he does, but what you are to do to keep your own will in a state conformable to nature, for another cannot hurt you unless you please. You will then be hurt when you consent to be hurt. In this manner, therefore, if you accustom yourself to contemplate the relations of neighbor, citizen, commander, you can deduce from each the corresponding duties. – Chapter 30, Epictetus' Enchiridion.

———

Returning to the concept of the roles that we play in life, Epictetus comments on this in a further developed manner. Generally, we know what we should do to fulfill the roles in our lives. Epictetus talks of them being universally known, but the society we live in really guides us on what we should be doing. We know what a good parent is, how children should act toward their parents, what it is to be a good sibling, and how we should be with our partners...neighbors...coworkers...anyone we interact with. We know inside of us how we should be properly playing those roles.

For this chapter, he mainly focuses on the relationship that we may have with our father. What are you supposed to do to be a good son or daughter? First, help take care of him (especially as he gets older) and patiently listen to how you have disappointed him and how he is trying to correct you. If you have a good father performing his role well, the corrections he is giving you are ways he is trying to help and impart his wisdom to you to improve your life and possibly avoid the mistakes he has made.

But what if your father is not a good one?

One thing for many of us in recovery is that we may not have had the best situations that we grew up in. We have stories of alcoholic or addict parents that were sometimes the root cause of the addictions that we were to suffer from. Even in my own life, I have had to look back on how my father's alcoholism affected my younger years and would partially influence the alcoholic I was to become. In many ways, I became exactly like my father when I was amid my addictions (he died before ever trying to live a life of recovery).

Does anyone have the right to a good father?

Epictetus points out one of the difficult things we must accept in life. No. Everyone has a father; you must have had one to be born. And the only thing that life can guarantee you is that you have the right to have a father. As for a good one...well, that cannot be so easily promised. We do not get to choose who our parents are...some people got good ones, and others not so good. Besides, we cannot change the past, and your parents being chosen is about as far into your past as you can go.

So, what do you do if your father (or mother) is not a good parent?

Well, you can still fulfill your duty as a son or daughter. You can still help your father or mother if they need help. It is within your power to do this and keeps you in your pursuit of excellence of character. You can still listen to their criticisms and disappointments, but I will point out Epictetus said you should patiently listen but do not necessarily have to believe. Remember what Epictetus had noted in earlier chapters on handling criticism in life. We should only listen to critics whose opinions we trust, and if you find that you have a parent that you cannot rely on, then their criticism should not matter.

Since studying Stoicism, I have had many conversations with people having difficulties with family members. Let's face it, most of our difficulties and "drama" in life come from them. I tell them you do your part to be a dutiful son or daughter and have completed what you intend to do. That person (the parent) not living up to their role is on them. At the end of the day, you get to sleep comfortably, knowing you did what was asked of you.

Epictetus then reminds us they cannot hurt you unless you allow them to. You decide if you will let their bad parenting get to you. It is a reminder to practice everything he has discussed about dealing with criticism, controlling your negative emotions, and not allowing someone to take ownership of your mind. Even though it is a parent you have to do this with, it does not make it any different from anyone else.

He finishes this by saying that we need to do this with all our roles in life. Brother or sister, friend, partner, coworker, or neighbor. And when you think of a neighbor, think of this in the sense of any person you can come across on any day. Remember that not only do we have no control over the people we come across in life, but at the same time, we do not know what is going on in their lives or minds to have them act the way they are. For all you know, there could be a valid reason they are behaving or performing their role in the way in which they are that day.

To understand this chapter fully, it is best to see how it further develops the concept of the grand universal play our births cast us in. Of course, when cast in a play, an actor is expected to perform to the best of their ability. It can be easy when others in the scene perform their roles well. It can be difficult when others perform poorly. However, the performance of others around the actor should have no bearing on whether or not they perform their role to the best of their ability. The expectation is that they should always do their best. It is why they were chosen.

It is why you were chosen for the grand universal play.

To be the best in every role you are given.

Ultimately, we know the duties that each role we play in life requires, and it is our duty to live up to them to the fullest. So even if the other person is not keeping up their end on the other side of the relationship, at least you get the peace of mind of knowing that you did what was right.

And your peace of mind is the most important thing.

"We play many roles in our life, but do we play each role intelligently and with a sense of responsibility? This is what we need to really ask ourselves." – Gurudev Sri Sri Ravi Shankar

CHAPTER 31

Stop Blaming God (Nature)
(Wisdom)

Be assured that the essence of piety toward the gods lies in this—to form right opinions concerning them, as existing and as governing the universe justly and well. And fix yourself in this resolution, to obey them, and yield to them, and willingly follow them amidst all events, as being ruled by the most perfect wisdom. For thus you will never find fault with the gods, nor accuse them of neglecting you. And it is not possible for this to be affected in any other way than by withdrawing yourself from things which are not within our own power, and by making good or evil to consist only in those which are. For if you suppose any other things to be either good or evil, it is inevitable that, when you are disappointed of what you wish or incur what you would avoid, you should reproach and blame their authors. – Chapter 31, Epictetus' Enchiridion.

W hen bad things happen in life, people often need to find a source on which to place that blame. And when it is difficult to pinpoint one exact person to point the finger at, it can be easy just to put that blame on God. And if you are not someone who believes in God, you might say that it is the world or universe that is working against you.

The first thing Epictetus points out in this chapter is that if you believe in God, then you also believe that he is good and rules the universe justly. And if all that happens is part of God's grand design, you should welcome the events that happen to you. But, on the other hand, if you do not believe in God, it would be ridiculous to think that the world is conspiring against you somehow when everything is merely cycles and patterns without a mind choosing who must deal with troubles in life and who does not. Therefore, if God is good and just with a master plan or a universe that runs through patterns and cycles, how could you blame them when things do not work out in the way you want them to?

Yes, bad things will happen to good people. And bad things will happen randomly. Although I will remind you how Stoics say it is a matter of judgment on seeing these things as being bad. However, Epictetus points out that we need to place the ideas of good and evil as being in our control rather than what is outside of our control.

Many of us in recovery have discovered the true meaning of this. During our addictions, we may have felt as if God or the universe were working against us.

Why do I have to live this life?

Why do things have to be this way?

Then what do we discover in our recovery? Many of the reasons our lives were not working out the way we wanted and many of those bad things were happening because of our actions. Good and evil lie in what we control. Not that God or the universe was conspiring to make our lives bad; we were the root cause of it. This is the primary purpose behind the fourth step in 12-step recovery programs, discovering your role in the problems you caused in life.

In the end, we need to realize that good and evil exist only within our choices and that we are the only ones we need to blame when things do not work out our way because of those choices. And if we continue to hold on to the idea that good and evil are in the things outside of our control, we will continue to blame God, the universe, or whoever we view as the cause of it. Which puts us at risk from seeing the role that we are playing in what happens, blinding ourselves to possibly seeing the actual root cause of what is occurring.

For many of us who have dealt with addictions, we know that blame is not healthy and could put our sobriety at risk. Therefore, instilling this concept of focusing on the good and evil within your control rather than what is outside of it will go a long way in helping your recovery.

———————

For every creature is naturally formed to flee and abhor things that appear hurtful and that which causes them; and to pursue and admire those which appear beneficial and that which causes them. It is impracticable, then, that one who supposes himself to be hurt should rejoice in the person who, as he thinks, hurts him, just as it is impossible to rejoice in the hurt itself. Hence, also, a father is reviled by his son when he does not impart the things which seem to be good; and this made Polynices and Eteocles mutually enemies—that empire seemed good to both. On this account the husbandman reviles the gods; [and so do] the sailor, the merchant, or those who have lost wife or child. For where our interest is, there, too, is piety directed. So that whoever is careful to regulate his desires and aversions as he ought is thus made careful of piety likewise. But it also becomes incumbent on everyone to offer libations and sacrifices and first fruits, according to the customs of his country, purely, and not heedlessly nor negligently; not avariciously, nor yet extravagantly. – Chapter 31, Epictetus' Enchiridion.

It is in the nature of all living things to hate the source of their harm while simultaneously pursuing the source of what they find beneficial. For example, how dogs or cats respond to people can be altered by how they are raised and the treatment they get in the process.

As living creatures, humans will show similar patterns of looking favorable to the source of what benefits them while having contempt for what brings harm. And sometimes, the anger inside us can be fed and flamed up by seeing someone or something standing in the way of what we want.

When we know the source of the hurt, it is easy to know where to direct our anger. For example, if a parent does not give their child what they want (or view as helpful), the child will turn their anger towards that parent. Polynices and Eteocles were brothers from Greek mythology who turned their hatred toward each other when they felt they should have the throne alone. Friends...family...coworkers... random people we come across. When we can justify why someone is standing in the way of what we need or delivering what we do not want, it gives a form of satisfaction to be able to put a name or face to direct our contempt.

But what if there is not a person to blame?

People often turn toward God or the universe to fill this void.

Farmers who had a lousy year with their crops. Sailors that were battling rough seas. Merchants losing their goods in transport. And people who lose their loved ones.

Even as I was writing this book, I heard a story in the news about the governor of Utah telling the people of the state to pray for rain to solve their water issues rather than looking into water conservation efforts. Who will they blame if the water issues continue and the rains do not come?

Epictetus highlights the sad reality that people let their view of God or the universe be guided by their own self-interest. They pray for the things they want to occur, as well as what they want to avoid. Then, if it works out their way, they praise like the animal pursuing what is helpful, and if it does not, they shout out blame or anger like the animal seeing something as harmful. Remember that the Lord's Prayer says "thy will be done" not "give me what I want." But even those who do not believe in God could find themselves in the trap of looking at the world with favorable eyes when things go their way and in spite when they do not.

This is not a healthy way of living.

This returns us to a concept discussed much earlier in the book. For the things we choose to desire and the things we choose to avoid, we need to choose wisely. We must keep what we want in life and what we want to avoid solely in the realm of what is in our control. We need to stay away from desiring what is outside of it. When we do this, we will never have a reason to blame another person, God, or the Universe, for things not going our way. Since we choose only what we have control over, we are the only ones to blame when circumstances do not happen in the manner we desire.

"Give up on your need to blame others for what you have or don't have, for what you feel or don't feel. Stop giving your powers away and start taking responsibility for your life." – Ritu Ghatourey

CHAPTER 32

Seeing Into the Future
(Wisdom)

When you have recourse to divination, remember that you know not what the event will be, and you come to learn it of the diviner; but of what nature it is you knew before coming; at least, if you are of philosophic mind. For if it is among the things not within our own power, it can by no means be either good or evil. Do not, therefore, bring with you to the diviner either desire or aversion—else you will approach him trembling—but first clearly understand that every event is indifferent and nothing to you, of whatever sort it may be; for it will be in your power to make a right use of it, and this no one can hinder. Then come with confidence to the gods as your counselors; and afterwards, when any counsel is given you, remember what counselors you have assumed, and whose advice you will neglect if you disobey. Come to divination as Socrates prescribed, in cases of which the whole consideration relates to the event, and in which no opportunities are afforded by reason or any other art to discover the matter in view. When, therefore, it is our duty to share the danger of a friend or of our country, we ought not to consult the oracle as to whether we shall share it with them or not. For though the diviner should forewarn you that the auspices are unfavorable, this means no more than that either death or mutilation or exile is portended. But we have reason within us; and it directs us, even with these hazards, to stand by our friend and our country. Attend, therefore, to the greater diviner, the Pythian God, who once cast out of the temple him who neglected to save his friend. – Chapter 32, Epictetus' Enchiridion.

Humans seem to have always wanted to know the future. To understand what is going to happen so that we can somehow prepare for it and come out favorably or at an advantage. For much of human history, we have relied on people with gifts to see into the future or diviners, as Epictetus describes them above. We still have people who practice this art, as you can visit a psychic, have your tarot cards read, or even read your horoscope to find out what to expect for you in the day ahead.

This desire to know what will happen in the coming days has continued into the technological era of humanity. Now we use computer algorithms and machine learning models that are fed data on what has happened in the past and the present to predict what the future will hold. They try to predict business sales months in advance, stock prices before they rise or fall, the weather days in advance, and even the outcome of sporting events days before they occur (for gambling). These same algorithms will try to predict what you want to buy before you have thought about it, what you want to eat before you plan your next meal, and where you want to travel to before you even plan your next vacation—all of this in an attempt to target you with advertisements to sway your opinion.

The more important discussion that is taking place in this chapter is on how we should view the future and how it should shape what we do. First, the future is one thing that lies in the realm of what we cannot control. It is out of our grasp. We can try to shape our future (saving money, going to college, making plans, etc.), but whether or not we have that future we aim for will involve many factors that we do not control. Even if you choose to go to someone that has the power to see into the future, these individuals have been found to be wrong at times. And even the most advanced machine learning models have an error rate that will describe the percentage of the time that the prediction will be wrong.

Knowing this unpredictability of the future, the Stoics would undertake any actions in the present with something that could be described as the 'reserve clause' (Robertson 2028, 122-123). The simple idea is that as they worked toward an outcome they desired, they would do it with this idea of the 'reserve clause' in mind, adding the caveat of "as long as nothing prevents me" or "fate permitting." So basically, as we commit actions in the present toward a future goal, we need to remind ourselves that the only way we attain that goal is if the things outside of our control do not impede achieving it.

Since the future is out of our control, it is something that we need to be indifferent to; it can be neither good nor bad. And no matter what the future holds, we can turn anything and everything in our favor. Therefore, always remember the challenges in life we face can do a lot to help shape who we are. No matter what you may learn about future events from a diviner or modern technology, it is still your responsibility to look at them with indifference to what they will mean for your life.

Epictetus then gives reasons why it is best not to know the future. He brings up what Socrates said about the subject. We do not need to talk to or consult anyone about the future if we can figure it out through reason alone. I find this humorous and insightful because many of us in recovery know exactly what this means. We do not need to talk to anyone about what would happen if we had that drink or just a little of the drug we crave. We already know what is going to happen. I am great at predicting the future. I will tell myself it is just one beer…I need another one since the buzz was not enough…maybe I need a couple of shots to get me to where I need to be…and days later, I wake up with a horrible hangover after a terrible bender.

My mind is good enough to predict the future.

It is also not good to know the future if you are bound by duty to something or someone since it might force you to hurt your character. For example, a soldier going off to war who knows that he will not come back alive may not act appropriately in battle then if he did not know this information. Or your friend is in a dangerous situation, and you need to get him out of it. It is best to play your part as a good friend and help without knowing what might happen to you. Some people gain secret knowledge of when a stock is about to skyrocket or plummet, and they use this information to buy or sell, which robs other people of money (the illegal act of insider trading). Sometimes it is best not to know the future when it will change how we act in the present and put the excellent character we are trying to develop in danger.

The future is what we make of it. It cannot be good or bad because it is in our power to turn it to our advantage. Sometimes we can predict the future ourselves (like having a bit of our drug of choice), and we should trust our instincts in those situations. But as humans continue to use technology to expand their ability to predict what will happen, we need to be cautious about what we learn. We need to make sure that no matter what we find out, it will not alter us from our path of virtuous character and that we still act correctly in each situation.

> "People ask me to predict the future, when all I want to do is prevent it. Better yet, build it. Predicting the future is much too easy, anyway. You look at the people around you, the street you stand on, the visible air you breathe, and predict more of the same. To hell with more. I want better." – Ray Bradbury, Beyond 1984: The People Machines.

CHAPTER 33

Ways in Which to Live Like a Stoic
(Courage, Justice, Temperance, Wisdom)

Begin by prescribing to yourself some character and demeanor, such as you may preserve both alone and in company.

Be mostly silent, or speak merely what is needful, and in few words. We may, however, enter sparingly into discourse sometimes, when occasion calls for it; but let it not run on any of the common subjects, as gladiators, or horse races, or athletic champions, or food, or drink—the vulgar topics of conversation—and especially not on men, so as either to blame, or praise, or make comparisons. If you are able, then, by your own conversation, bring over that of your company to proper subjects; but if you happen to find yourself among strangers, be silent. - Chapter 33, Epictetus' Enchiridion.

For this chapter, Epictetus lists the different ways you would put Stoic principles into practice in various life situations. It is this checklist of, now that you have learned what you have learned, then this is how you would apply it each day. Because the main point of

Stoicism is not just knowing it, but living it. This is why wisdom is just one virtue, and the other three are virtues of action.

He starts by saying that you need to choose the person you want to be and that you should be this person, whether you are around others or alone. Do not act one way in one situation and then differently in another. Our private and public lives should be completely indistinguishable from each other. You can sometimes hear people talking about this public and private face concept. That there are two forms to each person, one that they let everyone see and the true secret self that they keep hidden away from sight.

Many of us who have dealt with addiction know this concept too well. We had that public face we would bring outside the house to show the world. But at the same time, we were living a life of addiction and trying to hide that from the people who knew us (even though many of them could easily see it).

We were living two different lives.

The Stoics would say that this should not exist at all. There should only be one face (public and private) for any person. In recovery, we can no longer lead two different lives. We must learn to be honest about who we are to everyone we interact with. This even requires being honest about your addictions and your life of recovery (something that I have found to be quite empowering). Therefore, choose who you will be and live it at every moment, whether or not there are people around.

The second part of this chapter deals with how we should converse with others. One issue I had as an alcoholic was that I was often loud, annoying, and said too much when conversing (many things I should not be saying). Epictetus says we need to learn to live the opposite of this. To mainly remain silent, using our words sparingly when we feel the urge to. It is a "choose your words wisely" way of thinking. A famous quote associated with Epictetus says, "we are given one mouth and two ears for a reason." Basically, this implies that we should spend twice as much time listening to others as we spend speaking.

He continues his conversation discussion by saying that it is acceptable to enter them when the occasions call for it. Still, we should avoid conversations on common subjects like sports (gladiators, horse races, or athletic champions), food, or drink. Not that there is anything inherently wrong with these kinds of conversations; it is just that they are very superficial and lack the depth of truly meaningful conversation. And in life, we should desire to move away from the superficial parts of existence and seek true depth with those who we interact with.

Epictetus then points out that we definitely need to stay away from the vulgar conversations we have about other people. We should not engage in gossip about others. We should not cast judgments on other people. These kinds of conversations are opposite to the concept of Stoic justice, and if we find they are occurring in our presence, we should try to steer them away from these kinds of subjects. And if we cannot, we should not take part in them.

And finally, he says that if we find ourselves amongst a group of strangers, we should remain silent. This is not saying that you should never talk to strangers when amongst them; it is just an example of considering the situation. Sometimes you may find yourself amongst a group of strangers where talking is necessary (sobriety meetings, conferences, gatherings of friends, church, etc.). However, sometimes it is unnecessary. For example, I have a family member who will converse with people anywhere and everywhere—waiting in line, at drive-thru windows with workers, and anyone who sits next to them at any location. Not only are these going to be those superficial conversations that Epictetus said we should avoid, but at the same time, we do not even know if the stranger wants to take part in them. To force conversations on other people is to not consider their feelings, and they might only be speaking back out of kindness. You will not know if they want to participate or not unless they directly say it (which they most likely won't). Therefore, it is just best to stay silent when we find ourselves amongst a group of strangers.

———

Let not your laughter be loud, frequent, or abundant.

Avoid taking oaths, if possible, altogether; at any rate, so far as you are able.

Avoid public and vulgar entertainments; but if ever an occasion calls you to them, keep your attention upon the stretch, that you may not imperceptibly slide into vulgarity. For be assured that if a person be ever so pure himself, yet, if his companion be corrupted, he who converses with him will be corrupted likewise. – Chapter 33, Epictetus' Enchiridion.

———

Epictetus continues by advising not to be that person who laughs at everything and takes nothing seriously. And do not be that person who laughs so loud that you annoy everyone else around you. Not that the Stoics were anti-laughter and did not find things humorous. Remember that they want to promote the healthy emotions we can experience. He was mainly pointing out that people who are constantly making jokes or laughing will have a difficult time with people trying to take them seriously when they are trying to be. And we all need the opportunity to be taken seriously when the situations that call for it arise.

Try not to make promises; if you need to, make as few of them as possible. There is no reason to do this if you think about it. If you are going to do something, then do it; there is no real reason to promise to do it. Besides, many of us in recovery have made many promises to our loved ones during our addictions that they no longer have value to them. How many times have you sworn to loved ones that you would change or quit just to return to doing the same things?

They do not want promises; they just want action.

This section's last part is simply a warning about the company you keep. As we embark on this new journey as a philosopher and dedicate our life to virtuous living, we must know the people we keep company with. As we try to lift ourselves, we must be mindful of the people who can infect us and bring us back down. This is the exact reason they tell us to have our sober friends in recovery so we can have those with the same mind state as us to spend time with. If we continue to spend time around the same people with whom we had enjoyed our addictions, then there is quite a good chance that we will end up being brought down into our addictions once again. Radical changes in the lifestyle in which you live will not only be just about you as a person but will also have to flow out to the people who you surround yourself with.

Provide things relating to the body no further than absolute need requires, as meat, drink, clothing, house, retinue. But cut off everything that looks toward show and luxury.

Before marriage guard yourself with all your ability from unlawful intercourse with women; yet be not uncharitable or severe to those who are led into this, nor boast frequently that you yourself do otherwise. – Chapter 33, Epictetus' Enchiridion.

Stoics advocated for what we know today as the minimalist lifestyle. With the food you eat, the clothes you wear, the possessions you have, and the house you live in, seek to live a simple life, only having what is necessary.

Unfortunately, we live in a world dominated by designer brands and technological products that might seem exciting but are not essential. We are constantly bombarded with advertisements for things we need to own, foods we need to eat, and places we need to go. Companies are even using known psychological tricks that exploit human vulnerability to various forms of propaganda to trick you into buying more stuff and paying more for it (Lewis 2016). We are having psychological techniques used against us by companies to convince us we need whatever product they are selling, whether or not that may be true.

Minimalism is a mindset that looks at the things you own or are going to buy and to have you ask yourself if it is essential. For example, do you really need to replace your phone? Do you have to really eat at that restaurant? Does your car really need all of those features? For someone like me, who has lost everything I owned multiple times because of my addictions, it has been easy to discover what is necessary for my survival and what is not.

Minimalism has been a growing movement in recent years, with people finding the benefits being: saving more money, less stress, less time spent cleaning (the more you own, the more you have to take care of it), more time doing enjoyable activities, physical and mental health benefits, and it helps the environment (Kentucky Counseling Center 2021). It does not mean that you cannot have nice things, but it is more about thinking about the reason for the things you want or own. We need to look at the added value they bring to our lives and whether or not it is worth it for us to possess them. This should make sense for the Stoics since they say not to be ruled by our external possessions.

Furthermore, Stoic justice also comes into play when we follow the rapidly changing trends and the fast-fashion industry. Millions of tons of clothes from the fast fashion industry textile end up in countries like Ghana. Where it is dumped and is wreaking havoc on their environment and waterways (Choat 2023). This is just one example of how our actions deeply affect others, not to mention child labor, cheap and poor working conditions, and other human rights abuses carried out by the fashion brands we obsessively follow.

When it comes to sex, it is best to wait until marriage, but if you are going to have sex, then at least have it in a meaningful relationship (Stoics aren't that unrealistic about things). This is good advice for us in recovery, anyway. For some of us, we had destructive sexual relationships when we were amid our addictions. Therefore, it needs to be something we are careful about within our recovery.

But the other main points Epictetus is bringing up is to not look down on other people for the sexual choices that they make, even if they are contrary to how you think. Whoever someone else chooses to have sex with is up to them and should be of no concern to you. And if you are having sex, you should not go around boasting about it. By this point in the book, it should be apparent why he is saying this, as we have learned to hold back on our judgments of others and be humble in who we are.

———————

If anyone tells you that a certain person speaks ill of you, do not make excuses about what is said of you, but answer: "He was ignorant of my other faults, else he would not have mentioned these alone."

It is not necessary for you to appear often at public spectacles; but if ever there is a proper occasion for you to be there, do not appear more solicitous for any other than for yourself—that is, wish things to be only just as they are, and only the best man to win; for thus nothing will go against you. But abstain entirely from acclamations and derision and violent emotions. And when you come away, do not discourse a great deal on what has passed and what contributes nothing to your own amendment. For it would appear by such discourse that you were dazzled by the show. – Chapter 33, Epictetus' Enchiridion.

———————

I have already discussed internally how you should handle an insult from another person. But here, Epictetus presents an action you can do in that situation: Make a joke out of it.

"By laughing off an insult, we are implying that we don't take the insulter and his insults seriously. To imply this, of course, is to insult the insulter without directly doing so. It is therefore a response that is likely to deeply frustrate the insulter. For this reason, a humorous reply to an insult can be far more effective than a counterinsult would be." – William Irvine, A Guide to the Good Life, pg.148.

Epictetus points out that if someone insults you, rather than making an excuse or getting angry, say something like, "if he knew everything about me, he wouldn't have just said only that." Humor helps in two ways. First, it enables you to diffuse the situation and keeps you from acting out in anger. Second, it does not give the person the satisfaction they were aiming to get by insulting you. As William Irvine points out in his quote, it will probably be more frustrating to the insulter that you make a joke out of it rather than giving him the counterinsult he was expecting to get.

If you go to a sporting event, go with the attitude of let the best man...woman...team win. I know this one was difficult to think about when I first read it because I am an avid football fan and have my favorite team (Rams). At the moment that I am writing this, it is actually just a couple of weeks after the Rams beat the Bengals in the Super Bowl. But I remember telling myself before watching the game that I wanted the Rams to win, but it wouldn't be so bad if the Bengals won. It was nice to see what the Bengals had done in turning around their team that year. So, if they were the victors, it would not be such a terrible thing (plus, we always have next year...the sports fans' motto).

There are several reasons Epictetus discusses this. First, we often put our desire and aversion into the event's outcome when we watch sporting events. We have the team that we desire to win and want to see them avoid losing. We are putting desire and aversion in things entirely outside our control since we are not even taking part in the actual competition itself (and even if we were, it is not like the outcome would be entirely in our control anyway). And second, he understood what sports do to people by placing their desire and aversion into something out of their control. In countries worldwide, fans will fight verbally and physically with each other over the teams they love. I have lived in southern California all my life and attended many sporting events in Los Angeles, which can be notorious for fights in the seats. Even when the games end, the fighting will sometimes continue for days afterward (or even in the parking lots). For a philosophy that is trying to help with anger management, Epictetus realized he had to comment on sports (since it was obviously an issue during his time as well) and how we can watch them in a manner that will not cause us to be overcome with passion.

———

Be not prompt or ready to attend private recitations; but if you do attend, preserve your gravity and dignity, and yet avoid making yourself disagreeable.

When you are going to confer with anyone, and especially with one who seems your superior, represent to yourself how Socrates or Zeno would behave in such a case, and you will not be at a loss to meet properly whatever may occur. – Chapter 33, Epictetus' Enchiridion.

———

Meetings are an important part of the recovery process. And in this next part of the chapter, Epictetus is giving advice on how we should behave when it comes to them or any kind of speaking event that we attend if we feel the need to.

First, we need to keep our composure. I do not know about your experiences, but I have been to a few meetings where what was said caused someone to lose control of their emotions. It causes the whole gathering to turn in the wrong direction. It can ruin the experience for everyone that is there. Therefore, you need to make sure to maintain your composure at such events as these, sustaining your dignity through what is said. You do not want to be the one who ruins it for everyone else.

And of course, we find many different points of view and personalities within meetings. So, as you listen to people speak, do not listen with a mental state of disagreement. There is most likely a good chance that they are not Stoic, which means their perspectives are going to differ from yours. Instead, try to find the essence of what they are saying or use this as an opportunity to learn about them (since most of us attend the same meetings with the same people in attendance). And even if you disagree, be respectful and non-combative in how you choose to respond if you feel the need to. Really what Epictetus is trying to get at is how we should show proper respect to others with gatherings where people have speeches, another aspect of Stoic justice.

The next part of this chapter has Epictetus introducing the concept of the Stoic sage. In Stoicism, they felt it was a good practice to have that person you could call to mind for how you should act in any situation you are in. To have this concept of someone who is perfectly wise and good gives the aspiring Stoic direction, structure, and consistency in practice (Robertson 2018, 112). It is very similar in concept to the idea of WWJD (What Would Jesus Do) that became popular among Christians years ago.

The Stoic sage is an individual that has perfected the practice of the philosophy, following it at all times and in all kinds of situations perfectly. It is often thought among Stoics that an individual will most likely never attain this level within their own life, which means that you will most likely never meet one in person. We are all human, which means that we will all have errors from time to time. Basically, it is always progress in this philosophy with an understanding that perfection will never be fully attained. But having the vision of the Stoic sage to refer to gives us a perfect mentor for what we should be doing in any situation.

What Epictetus suggests doing here is that whenever you go to get the opinion from someone, especially those who may seem superior, do this by thinking of how Socrates or Zeno (the founder of Stoicism) would behave in that situation. Just because you may see this person as superior does not mean what they say will be correct. Therefore, he suggests you approach these situations with the different aspects of Stoic practice and mind-states that have been discussed as you think of how the sage would act to see what is learned or gained from the situation appropriately.

When you are going before anyone in power, fancy to yourself that you may not find him at home, that you may be shut out, that the doors may not be opened to you, that he may not notice you. If, with all this, it be your duty to go, bear what happens and never say to yourself, "It was not worth so much"; for this is vulgar, and like a man bewildered by externals.

In company, avoid a frequent and excessive mention of your own actions and dangers. For however agreeable it may be to yourself to allude to the risks you have run, it is not equally agreeable to others to hear your adventures. Avoid likewise an endeavor to excite laughter, for this may readily slide you into vulgarity, and, besides, may be apt to lower you in the esteem of your acquaintance. Approaches to indecent discourse are likewise dangerous. Therefore, when anything of this sort happens, use the first fit opportunity to rebuke him who makes advances that way, or, at least, by silence and blushing and a serious look show yourself to be displeased by such talk. – Chapter 33, Epictetus' Enchiridion.

———————

Epictetus returns to the concept of the reserve clause discussed in the previous chapter. He outlines how we should approach the people who may have power or control over something that might be our goal. His main advice is that we need to be prepared for things not to go our way (returning to the idea of premeditation of evil or troubles). For example, we may find that the person may not be reached or possibly even refuse to speak with us, or they may not even notice that we exist. If we will accept these negative outcomes and still find it worth our time, then we should proceed with what we will do. And if things go our way, then that is awesome. However, if they do not, we see this as a learning experience (Stoic challenge) and should never think we wasted our time doing what we did.

This part helped me with the new career path that I embarked on. One piece of advice some people often give is that about a week after applying for a job, try to contact the hiring manager or maybe even someone at the company to get your foot in the door and your resume seen. This requires sometimes reaching out to people who do not know you but have the power to get you noticed among the stack of resumes. Sometimes they will reply positively...sometimes negatively...and often no contact at all. But each time, I improved in what I wrote and how I approached the next person I would contact. I learned what they were looking for in what I wrote and which people were the best ones to contact to achieve my results of getting a positive reply. My goal was to make contact in order to get a job if something out of my control (the other person I was contacting) did not get in the way, and I never took it personal if they did not respond favorably if at all; I chose to learn from each one.

In the last part of this chapter, Epictetus discusses some things we should avoid when starting conversations with other people. First, he says we should avoid excessively discussing the adventures and dangers we have experienced. This can be an essential point for those of us in recovery. Yes, it can sometimes be good to discuss the things that we have gone through in our addictions, and this can help get people to understand their own addictions, but we also need to be aware of the fact that we can sometimes trigger people with the things that we say as well. Beyond addiction, people rarely like a person who excessively feels the need to talk about themselves and their lives; it reflects narcissism and self-absorption that is opposite to the Stoic way of thinking.

We also need to be cautious in conversations that might be vulgar or inappropriate. First, it might make the people we are talking with feel uncomfortable with what we are saying. Second, it could cause people to think less of us. And I know the Stoics feel we should not care about the reputation that others give to us since it is out of our control, but we should not be making efforts on our own part to destroy it.

Throughout this chapter, Epictetus takes a moment in which he takes these big ideas he has discussed about the Stoic perspective on life and gives specific examples of how they would be used in your daily living. It is an example of what they call putting theory into practice. Of course, many other aspects of life will change if you choose to live as a Stoic, but this gives you a good starting point on where to begin.

"You will never plough a field if you only turn it over in your mind." – Irish Proverb

CHAPTER 34

Dealing With Temptation
(Temperance)

If you are dazzled by the semblance of any promised pleasure, guard yourself against being bewildered by it; but let the affair wait your leisure, and procure yourself some delay. Then bring to your mind both points of time—that in which you shall enjoy the pleasure, and that in which you will repent and reproach yourself, after you have enjoyed it—and set before you, in opposition to these, how you will rejoice and applaud yourself if you abstain. And even though it should appear to you a seasonable gratification, take heed that its enticements and allurements and seductions may not subdue you, but set in opposition to this how much better it is to be conscious of having gained so great a victory. – Chapter 34, Epictetus' Enchiridion.

Self-control is essential to Stoics. It is why temperance is one of the four core virtues. They realize that when we do not have self-control, we will think less rationally about our decisions, which will cause us to make bad choices that will lead to negative emotions (regret, shame, etc.) and can have harmful repercussions on our life.

It is one of the major ways in which Stoicism can benefit individuals who have struggled with addiction. We are people with a past in which we could not practice self-control. Therefore, gaining this ability is essential for a strong recovery.

If you find yourself tempted by some form of pleasure, that needs to be a sign for you to put your guard up. It could be any pleasure that we know we should not be doing. The thought of that one drink or one hit. It could be a chance to have sex even though we shouldn't (like cheating on a partner). An opportunity to get away with stealing. Or it could even be as simple as cheating on a diet you are dedicated to. Just because you may no longer be partaking in your drug of choice does not mean that you will never meet any temptations again.

So, what should you do when confronted with temptation?

First, you need to buy yourself a moment to think.

Second, think about how long you will enjoy that pleasure. How long will you enjoy that drink or hit? How long will the pleasures of sex last? How long will you enjoy getting away with what you took? How long will you enjoy eating that food that breaks your diet?

Third, think of how long the guilt or shame of giving in to that pleasure will last. In a small version of "playing the tape forward," how will you feel as soon as the pleasure is gone? It could be that same day, the next morning, or after an extended bender. Anyone who has relapsed can easily recall what they felt when they came down. And if you have not relapsed, think of anything wrong you did and how it made you feel when the pleasure was gone.

Finally, compare the amount of time for the two situations and ask yourself if it will be worth it. Will that small amount of time you have pleasure giving into temptation be worth the extended time you might have to feel guilt, shame, or regret? It is kind of ridiculous if you ever think about the self-inflicted shame and regret that we can sometimes punish ourselves with for just a moment of pleasure. Every time I relapsed, the amount of time I had to endure the shame and regret I felt after I gave in increased exponentially.

Epictetus finishes this chapter off with one last argument. Let's say that you have compared the times, and you still feel that it would benefit you more to give into temptation. You need to ask yourself how it will feel for you not to give in. To have victory over temptation. Remember those early days of sobriety when every single day was a reason to celebrate? I think this is why they give out so many chips in those early days, because the battle over temptation is genuinely at its strongest, and each day without giving in is indeed a hard-fought day.

"Everyone must choose one of two pains: The pain of discipline or the pain of regret." – Jim Rohn

In the end, when faced with temptation, you have two options: giving in or staying away. To give in will bring to you that brief moment of pleasure seductive glances of temptation offers, as well as the more extended moments of negative emotions that follow. On the other hand, staying away may steal that brief moment of pleasure, but it also delivers powerful positive emotions of conquering temptation, destroying any possible negative emotions that giving in would have brought.

From here on out, when faced with temptation, practice this mental balancing of the timesheets for giving in or letting go. And always note the significant difference between these two in terms of time and emotional effects. Over time, you should discover yourself doing fewer regretful actions while increasing more that you are proud of.

"Every conquering temptation represents a new fund of moral energy. Every trial endured and weathered in the right spirit makes a soul nobler and stronger than it was before." – William Butler Yeats

CHAPTER 35

Courage in What You Do
(Courage)

When you do anything from a clear judgment that it ought to be done, never shrink from being seen to do it, even though the world should misunderstand it; for if you are not acting rightly, shun the action itself; if you are, why fear those who wrongly censure you? – Chapter 35, Epictetus' Enchiridion.

By this point of the book, I have discussed many of the core concepts of Stoicism:

- Focus on what you control and put less value on those things outside of it.
- Remember to judge things properly as they should be; they are not bad or good; they just simply are.
- Ways we should handle the actions and words that come from other people.
- We all have roles in this world, and it is our job to be the best at fulfilling them.
- Humanity is on this planet united to care for each other.

Using this knowledge and thinking rationally, if you conclude that something is right, do it no matter what anyone else says. One thing to understand about living the life of a Stoic is you have to accept that you will live in a way in which most people do not. This should be easy to see with how much I have explained all the different ways you approach the world and life as a Stoic philosopher. Therefore, sometimes you will do things you know are the right things you should do, but since the world has a different set of values, they may not understand why.

I think one of the fundamental ways we can see the essence of this chapter playing out in recovery is the amends-making process that many of us go through. Some people may wonder why we would return to people we have wronged in the past (some people we may have not even spoken to in years) and repay debts that we might have owed them. Some people may wonder why waste the time or money. But for those in recovery, we know that we must do this because it is the right thing to do and must be done. It becomes an essential part of our growth in the new life we choose to live after addiction.

We need to learn that doing the right thing is the only reasoning that we need behind the actions we commit to. The thoughts and views of others in the process should no longer matter. This is something easily possible for us. Many addicts had no issue with continuing their addiction despite the wishes of others. So now we can use that same mind state but use it for good rather than evil.

Epictetus ends this chapter simply by saying that if you know deep down inside that you should not be doing something, you should not do it whether or not people agree with you. However, if you know that this is something you should do, that it is the actions of someone showing the excellence of character, then you should do it no matter what anyone says, because they might live by different values than you have. Besides, why fear what anyone should say when you know what you are doing is right and the only opinion that matters is your opinion of yourself?

"To see what is right, but to fail to do it, is to be lacking in courage." – Confucius, The Analects, 2.24.

CHAPTER 36

Consideration of Others
(Justice)

As the proposition, "either it is day or it is night," has much force in a disjunctive argument, but none at all in a conjunctive one, so, at a feast, to choose the largest share is very suitable to the bodily appetite, but utterly inconsistent with the social spirit of the entertainment. Remember, then, when you eat with another, not only the value to the body of those things which are set before you, but also the value of proper courtesy toward your host. – Chapter 36, Epictetus' Enchiridion.

The Stoics always wanted to present the logic behind why we should do certain things. In this chapter, Epictetus focuses on why we cannot be selfish and selfless simultaneously. We can have one or the other, but not both together.

A disjunctive argument is one in which you have two distinct options that cannot happen simultaneously, while a conjunctive argument is one in which you can have both at the same time. Epictetus presents a simple example to understand the difference between the two. "Either it is day, or it is night" would be a disjunctive argument since you can only have one and not the other occurring at the same moment. It cannot be conjunctive because we cannot have day and night together.

He then returns to the idea of a feast he has used throughout this book. At a feast, you can have as much as you desire to eat, but everything you consume cannot be consumed by the other people attending. Yes, it might be good for you and your body to eat most of the food, but what will that mean for the needs of others at the feast? The more that you have, the less that there is for others. Therefore, this is a disjunctive situation since two people cannot eat the same food.

This is how the concept of selfishness and selflessness is presented; they are disjunctive ideas. You cannot be selfish and want everything for yourself while being selfless and considerate of others. You have to choose which one you will be and not lie to yourself that you can have both.

This returns us to the concept of the sphere of control. In our addictions, we often lived lives that were quite selfish. Not only is the act of addiction selfish in its own right, but it also causes us to try to control the world around us to deal with the lack of self-control. And in our recovery, we need to shed this life of selfishness and live selfless lives. We cannot mesh these two together because they are just as disjunctive as day and night are.

They are polar opposites.

We need to treat our interactions with others as if we are at this feast of life. We can't have everything the way we want and all for ourselves while treating others properly. So, we need to be courteous to others and share the food of life equally.

Be considerate of your partner and their feelings…be equals. Do not demand that conversation is about what you want to talk about, but let others speak their desires (listen more than speak). Accept that everything cannot be how you want it to be and that others should have their needs met as well.

Releasing your need to control everything in life will have fantastic positive effects throughout your days. You will no longer have to deal with the frustrations of everything not going the way that you want it to. Conflicts with others will decrease dramatically as they feel validated and nourished. Relationships with others will become deeper and more meaningful. And you now are living for others rather than just yourself (Stoic justice).

"Personal growth is the torturous journey from selfishness to selflessness." – VK Madhav Mohan

CHAPTER 37

Do What You Do Best
(Courage, Justice, Wisdom)

If you have assumed any character beyond your strength, you have both demeaned yourself ill in that and quitted one which you might have supported. – Chapter 37, Epictetus' Enchiridion.

Years ago, I used to work as a teacher (although my raging alcoholism would affect my ability to continue). One of the funny sayings in the world is, "Those who can't do, teach." It implies that people who cannot do whatever subject they studied in the real world become teachers. But it also suggests that anyone can teach. In all my years of teaching (almost a decade), I can say this idea is truly wrong. As a teacher, I came across many people so natural at the art of teaching. And I met others that just did not have it in them. I witnessed several people quit the profession quickly as they discovered they did not have what it takes inside of them to teach successfully. I even remember one person who quit two months into his first year of teaching as he realized it was much more difficult than he had expected. Some of you may know this personally. You might have had those teachers who were amazing at what they did and made it so easy to learn…and then you might have had those teachers who were just so bad at it that you couldn't learn anything.

Some characters or roles we take on in this grand universal play of life are of our own choosing. One of these can be the jobs or careers that we choose. Now, I know that sometimes you might have to do any job that you can get. This can be especially true early in recovery, as we might have destroyed our chances of continuing our past careers from our addictions, like what I did with my ability to teach. The only job I could find when I got out of rehab was working the grill at a fast-food restaurant, despite having multiple college degrees.

Some people talk about the idea that you can do whatever you want in life if you put your mind to it and do not give up. Stoics would not believe this…they are a bit more realistic. They realize that there are just some things a person cannot do. For example, I could never be an opera singer…I do not have the voice for it. In my younger years, I could not be a track star since I did not have the speed. And even though I studied biology, I could not be a brain surgeon because of my Tourette's tics. I am pretty twitchy and move a lot, which would not go well for long hours of surgery.

> "We do not 'come into' this world; we come out of it, as leaves from a tree. As the ocean 'waves,' the universe 'peoples.' Every individual is an expression of the whole realm of nature, a unique action of the total universe." – Alan Watts, The Book: On the Taboo Against Knowing Who You Are, pg. 9.

Every person is a unique expression of the universe. We came out of the universe and are a part of the patterns and cycles that flow through it. The universe chose it was this moment and this time that you were to exist and that it needs you. Everyone has a purpose to fulfill and a reason they are needed.

Two things will happen when you choose a role to fulfill in life that you are not fit for. First, you are going to punish yourself. You will be demeaned or embarrassed. You will deal with negative emotions constantly. The teachers that I watched discover that they were not fit for the career would have to deal with emotional brutality almost daily to the point of breaking (I heard about one teacher that the students could get to cry anytime they felt like it). And on top of that, those teachers then cannot properly instruct, negatively impacting the lives of every student they come into contact with.

Second, you rob the world and the universe of your true purpose. As you were chosen to exist at this moment in the universe's history, you were chosen for something that the world needs you to do. When you do the thing that is your strength, a role meant for you, then you create a positive change for every person you interact with as you make the world a better place.

I will never forget a conversation with the principal at the first school I worked at. She was discussing how her father loved working in custodial services (something the world definitely needs), and it was truly what he was meant to do. Because of that, he excelled in the position so much that he was running his own custodial services company and was doing better in life than she was (monetarily wise). An essential job much needed by the world that many people would not want to do became a major success for her father since it was a passion of his.

That is the other side of it. When you truly set your sights on the best role for your abilities, you will find less struggle and more excellence. More positive emotions than negative ones. You are making the world and humanity better by what you do rather than taking from them.

And this does not have to be solely about your chosen career. We can decide other roles that we will play in life as well. Do you have what it takes to be a good parent, or would you serve the world better by not having children? It takes more courage to admit that you possibly do not have the ability to be a good parent to any children you may choose to have than to go ahead and just have them and possibly ruin their lives. Can you continue to be a good partner with the person you are with, or would it be better if you separated or divorced? My parents would spend their entire time together, never admitting that it would be better if they separated (due to different sets of values) which led to misery for both of them and me and my brother. Would you be a good sponsor for a particular person, or should you help their recovery by guiding them toward someone who would be more fit? Sponsoring someone is an admirable honor, but doing this with someone who may not match well with you could put their recovery at risk. Even though an opportunity for a role comes into your life does not mean that you have to jump at the chance to take it. Always see that there could be other options and think about what would work best for your abilities as well as for other people. Another way in which to practice Stoic justice.

Some of us in recovery question the paths we have taken in life and our past choices. As you move forward in this new life of recovery, ask yourself if the roles of your choice come from your weaknesses or strengths. Think about what you can give to this world because of your unique being. And use this understanding to choose the roles you will perform in the universal play to the best of your ability.

The universe chose you.

The world needs you.
Choose wisely.

"Choose a job you love, and you will never have to work a day in your life." – Author unknown

CHAPTER 38

Protect Your Mind
(Temperance, Wisdom)

As in walking you take care not to tread upon a nail, or turn your foot, so likewise take care not to hurt the ruling faculty of your mind. And if we were to guard against this in every action, we should enter upon action more safely. – Chapter 38, Epictetus' Enchiridion.

In this chapter, Epictetus again brings together several concepts he has brought up throughout this book to synthesize them from a different perspective. He again points out how we are so careful and cautious with our bodies. We do so much to ensure we do not harm our bodies as we do different things throughout the day. We wear shoes to protect our feet as we walk. Seatbelts as we drive around with cars with various safety features in case of an accident. Warning signs everywhere that there could be some form of danger. Humanity has realized the body's importance for survival and the need to protect it when harm could come.

However, we neglect to protect our thoughts and rational mind.

It is kind of funny when you think about it in a way. Our mind determines what we are doing throughout the entire day. Yet, we do not consider the importance of protecting our thoughts the same way we do our bodies. Ultimately, it is our mind that is going to determine what our body is going to end up doing. How many times have you caused harm to your body because of a poorly thought-out action? Therefore, one of the best ways to protect your body is to protect your mind and what it is thinking and then tell your body what to do.

Our minds are attacked daily. Think of all the things that happen to you on any given day that could cause negative emotions that cloud your ability to think straight. Think of all the things that cause you to lose focus on what you are doing. And when we have lost control of our rational mind, we risk putting our lives and bodies in danger. Therefore, we must keep our guard and protect our rational minds and thoughts from being attacked so we do not lose our grip on them.

How do we do this?

By synthesizing the ideas discussed in this book.

Are you thinking irrationally because of something that is out of your control? You need to practice acceptance. Are you losing your mind because something bad has happened? You need to learn to remove value judgments from events. Has something triggered that first involuntary reflex of anger? You need to take a moment to regain control of your thoughts. And above all else, see any difficulty as a Stoic challenge and an opportunity to grow.

The better that you guard your mind, the better you will be at determining the actions you will do. Emotions or passions won't carry you away. You will do fewer things that you regret and have to apologize for. There will be fewer things you do that could endanger your body. You will be surer that what you do is the right thing to do in any situation. You will enter into action more safely.

Your mind is a part of your body.

In many ways, the most important.

Guard it at all times.

"A man who has not clarity of mind has nothing." – Kamil Gupta

CHAPTER 39

Never Enough
(Temperance)

The body is to everyone the proper measure of its possessions, as the foot is of the shoe. If, therefore, you stop at this, you will keep the measure; but if you move beyond it, you must necessarily be carried forward, as down a precipice; as in the case of a shoe, if you go beyond its fitness to the foot, it comes first to be gilded, then purple, and then studded with jewels. For to that which once exceeds the fit measure there is no bound. – Chapter 39, Epictetus' Enchiridion.

In this chapter, Epictetus returns to the concept of minimalism and its importance in life. He discusses that the body is the perfect measure of what we need to survive. If you can focus mainly on making sure that what you have are the basic needs in life, then you will keep yourself in check. But the more you move beyond this, the more your desires have the chance of growing insatiable and wanting more and more and more.

He uses the example of a foot. A foot needs a good shoe to cover it for getting around. But what happens if your desires grow beyond just having a simple shoe? He says...maybe you will want it to be gold...but that is not enough...now you want it purple (a sign of royalty or status to Romans)...but now that is not enough...now you want it covered with jewels. But what happens when you tire of the jewels? What will you want next?

Seneca described this situation perfectly when he said:

"Nature's wants are slight; the demands of opinion are boundless. Suppose that the property of many millionaires is heaped up in your possession. Assume that fortune carries you far beyond the limits of a private income, decks you with gold, clothes you in purple, and brings you to such a degree of luxury and wealth that you can bury the earth under your marble floors; that you may not only possess, but tread upon, riches. Add statues, paintings, and whatever any art has devised for the luxury; you will only learn from such things to crave still greater.

Natural desires are limited; but those which spring from false opinion can have no stopping-point. The false has no limits. When you are travelling on a road, there must be an end; but when astray, your wanderings are limitless." – Seneca, Letters from a Stoic, Letter 16.

What we need for our survival is not very much. A good enough place to live in...not a massive mansion with more bedrooms and bathrooms than the people living in it can use. A car that meets our needs for getting around...not an overpriced luxury car. Clothes that match our needs to cover ourselves in the environment that we are in...not luxury brands that are just higher priced for the label on them.

Seneca and Epictetus are saying that the problem becomes when you think you need more than your basic needs. Once you wander down the path of the opinion that you need higher-priced luxurious possessions that go beyond nature, there will be no end to your desires. There will always be something "better" that you can get.

I remember watching an interview once online where this man was talking about how his life goal was to get a Lamborghini, and once he did, he would feel like he was wealthy and accomplished. And he got that Lamborghini. However, a little bit later, he saw more expensive and "nicer" ones than his, and all he could think about was how the one he had was not good enough. He needed a better one. Using society's opinion on what kind of car reflects wealth led to him wanting even more once he had achieved the original goal that he had laid out for himself.

> *"We humans are unhappy in large part because we are insatiable; after working hard to get what we want, we routinely lose interest in the object of our desire. Rather than feeling satisfied, we feel a bit bored, and in response to this boredom, we go on to form new, even grander desires. The psychologists Shane Frederick and George Loewenstein have studied this phenomenon and given it a name: hedonic adaptation."* – William B. Irvine, The Guide to the Good Life, pg. 66.

The basic idea behind hedonic (relating to pleasant sensations) adaptation is that we, as humans (like other living organisms), are made to adapt to our environments; it is the essence of survival. So, when we go through life changes, we will adapt to those changes, including the things we possess. When we finally achieve something we desire, we will eventually adapt to having it in our lives. It becomes a part of the regular environment that we are used to. This can include the things that you buy, the relationships that you have, and the job that you go to.

Using the example of the Lamborghini above. He had wanted and desired that car and looked at it as the end all be all of what he wanted when it was not a part of his regular environment. When he finally got it, he was probably happy for a while. However, as time passed by, he adapted to having that car in his possession, so the happiness he got from it decreased. Finally, it became just a normal part of his environment. So, he turned his attention to what he could get next that would give him happiness (a better Lamborghini).

Hedonic adaptation happens to pretty much all people, addict or not. Think of how you may have landed your dream job and found happiness over having it fade over time. Or you may have gotten into that relationship with someone you had been aching to be with to find the pleasure you were getting from it reducing as the days passed. Or maybe it was simply something you had set your sights on buying just to find out that it wasn't as enjoyable as you initially thought after a while.

In essence, it is the mind of an addict. The drug is happiness. Getting something gives us that high of happiness that we want, but like any drug, we crash after some time and then turn our attention to where we can find our next hit.

There was a point in my life when I had a family (wife and daughter), a two-story house, a car, a career, and many things I desired to own. Everything I could imagine myself wanting in life in my younger years. However, as time passed, I discovered that this was not enough. I adapted to having the wife in my life. I adapted to the career...the car...the house...everything. And as I adapted to having these things in my environment, I was getting less joy out of having them, which led me to look for new ways to get that high of happiness again.

I have heard this story from many people in recovery; they had everything they thought they wanted but still did not feel fulfilled. Unfortunately, drugs and alcohol, for many of us that have had this feeling, became that outlet for the lack of fulfillment.

However, now in recovery, we must live life differently. After a little bit of sobriety, it is easy to fall back into that trap again, thinking about all those things we had lost and how if we could get them back again, it would be different this time. But we need to be cautious. As I stated above, hedonic adaptation is acting like an addict and happens to everyone, so we have to be careful with its effect on us.

We need to keep ourselves in check. Our body is the perfect gauge for what we need to survive, and those needs are minimal. Our possessions are externals we cannot give control to because if we do, they will keep pushing us further and further till we find ourselves going over a cliff. Remember, negative visualization (imagining losing the things that you have) and the power it has to build appreciation. It is a tool to combat hedonic adaptation. Rather than losing the joy you are getting out of the things in your life by adapting to them, it pushes you to think of your environment without them to continue that happiness.

Ultimately, it is all about asking yourself what you truly need to survive and being honest with yourself. And then fighting back hedonic adaptation by building a greater appreciation of what you have at this moment right now rather than living like an addict looking for another hit.

"My riches consist, not in the extent of my possessions, but in the fewness of my wants." – Joseph Brotherton

CHAPTER 40

Stoicism Is for Everyone
(Justice, Wisdom)

Women from fourteen years old are flattered by men with the title of mistresses. Therefore, perceiving that they are regarded only as qualified to give men pleasure, they begin to adorn themselves, and in that to place all their hopes. It is worth while, therefore, to try that they may perceive themselves honored only so far as they appear beautiful in their demeanor and modestly virtuous. – Chapter 40, Epictetus' Enchiridion.

The more things change, the more they stay the same. We want to think that as humanity progresses in knowledge and technology, our society and the values we hold near and dear have also progressed. However, it never ceases to amaze me as I have read the works of the Ancient Stoics and other philosophers that it does not appear so. Instead, humanity behaves in ways today that are so similar to how we behaved thousands of years ago.

Young women often learn that their appearance is more important than who they are. As they enter their teenage years, the attention they get from boys and men for their appearance can make a young lady see that as her most valuable asset. In response, some women emphasize their appearance as they dress differently and wear more makeup. It is a telling sign that the American Society of Plastic Surgeons reports that 92% of all cosmetic surgeries in America in 2020 were for women (ASPS 2020). Women feel the need to change the way they look and enhance their appearance at a rate astronomically higher than men do.

Social media is just making the problem worse. Through likes, follows, and comments, women can now gauge the value of their appearance through their posts. Teenage boys tend to share funny and entertaining posts, while teenage girls tend to share posts that try to present themselves with how they want to be seen (Northwestern 2020). These differences have led to a more significant impact on teenage girls' mental health, as they have been found to have higher rates of depression and body image issues when compared to teenage boys. It is kind of twisted if you think about it. We have advanced technologically so much just to find more efficient ways to convey the idea to women that how they look is their most important asset.

I struggle with this knowledge since I have a teenage daughter. She is an extraordinary person. She is funny, caring, intelligent, well-spoken, thoughtful, and has a powerful mind. Thinking of a world that would tell her that only how she looks is her most valuable asset would wrong the person she is. As a father, I am doing my part to show her that her value lies within her, but as many things are with Stoicism, I am only trying to instill something in her that the world promotes differently.

"It is obvious that there is not one type of virtue for a man and another for a woman.

If men and women must be equally good in the virtue appropriate for a human...will we not educate both alike, and teach both the same way the art by which a human would become good? We must do just that!" – Musonius Rufus, Lecture 4.

The Ancient Stoics did not see that philosophy was only something for men. There are arguments about whether the Stoics were some of the first feminists, and I will not get into that. But the one obvious thing is that they saw being a philosopher as something for all of humanity and not just for men. The virtues that make a person good and lead a life of excellence do not change by gender.

Our appearance is external to us. It is out of our control. Every single one of us is one accident away from altering how we look for the rest of our lives. It happens to people every single day. However, no calamity can change who we are as a person unless we let it do so.

As Epictetus is saying in this chapter, women need to learn and know that the true beauty they will have is not superficial but in how they act and the virtuous nature that they contain. It does not do any person good to be beautiful on the outside while remaining ugly on the inside. Therefore, as Musonius was saying, men and women need to learn philosophy in the same way to be equally good at the virtues a human should have.

In other words, Stoicism is for everyone! This book and its lessons for recovery are equally applicable for women as they are for men. Anyone, despite their gender, race, color, or bank balance can benefit from these teachings.

"I hate to hear you talk about all women as if they were fine ladies instead of rational creatures. None of us want to be in calm waters all our lives." – Jane Austen, Persuasion.

CHAPTER 41

Workout Your Mind
(Wisdom)

It is a mark of want of intellect to spend much time in things relating to the body, as to be immoderate in exercises, in eating and drinking, and in the discharge of other animal functions. These things should be done incidentally and our main strength be applied to our reason. – Chapter 41, Epictetus' Enchiridion.

———————

This one is for the addicts.

And those of us in recovery know it all too well.

A few chapters ago, Epictetus discussed how we could be so cautious when protecting our bodies, but not so much when protecting the ruling faculty of our mind. In this chapter, he further expands on this concept by discussing the immoderate time that we do things for the body while spending less time working on our mind's ability to reason (think logically). To the Stoics, this is odd, mainly because we can see the body lying in the realm of something we rarely have control over, while the mind is the one thing we always do.

Epictetus focuses on three main things that people can spend more time than necessary doing: exercising, eating and drinking, and the discharge of animal functions (a nice way of saying sex but can also include going to the bathroom). The thing that I find interesting about these examples is that they all can lead to their own forms of addiction. And I know that exercise may not seem like a form of addiction (although anything can be an addiction if you do it too much), but studies have found that the use of steroids correlates with individuals that go to the gym more than those that do not (Leifmen et al. 2018). So, in a way, Epictetus noted that people, even during his time, seemed to be addicted and spending more time than necessary for these activities for the body than was actually required.

Beyond people who are addicted to these things of the body, you can see the emphasis on these activities in general among humans. Go on any social media site, and you can find people creating posts of themselves at the gym or of the food and drinks they consume. And everyone is quite aware of the prevalence of pornography online. The Stoics are not prudish and anti all these things. Epictetus points out that these are obvious needs for the body, but what are we doing for our minds? Are we spending as much time working out, eating and drinking, and having sex as we are doing things to strengthen our minds and our abilities to think logically? How much effort are you putting into working out your mind daily?

An essential reason for cultivating this mindset is that it demands level-headedness and rational thinking in our daily lives. To embody the Stoic philosophy to its fullest, we must engage in continuous strength training of the mind. As emphasized throughout this book, the Stoic way of thinking may sharply contrast with what we've grown accustomed to throughout our lives. As a result, it requires dedicated mental training to become proficient at it.

Adopting Stoic principles can be a transformative experience, but it does not happen overnight. To integrate these teachings into our lives effectively, we must strengthen our mental faculties, embrace reason, and practice resilience in the face of life's challenges. With time and consistent effort, we can cultivate the Stoic mindset and navigate the complexities of existence with greater wisdom and tranquility.

The funny thing is that those in recovery know why this chapter exists and its importance. It is not like we can just quit our drug of choice and be done entirely with it. The problem was not the drug; it was our way of thinking. Stinking thinking is the term that is used for it. Quitting the drug is just the beginning; it is the changing of our minds that will lead to long-term recovery. This is why going to rehab programs, attending meetings, and reading recovery literature is recommended for a stronger recovery. We need to hear from others and learn new ways of approaching the world to alter our minds from remaining on the same paths that lead to our addictions.

If you look back on many of the Stoic practices that have been discussed in this book, they are all ways you can workout your mind. To remove judgments from events, consider the things in your control and out of your control, practice negative visualization, and take part in Stoic challenges are all mental activities that will strengthen your ability to think rationally.

"Allow not sleep to close your wearied eyes, until you have reckoned up each daytime deed: 'Where did I go wrong? What did I do? And what duty's left undone?" – Epictetus, Discourses, 3.10 2-3.

Another way the Stoics advocated to workout the mind in a healthy way is very similar to Step 10. Each night we need to look back on the day in which we had just lived and think about what we did right and what we did wrong. Reflect on how we practiced the Stoic principles and how we might have dropped the ball and could have done better. This could be done by mentally going over it in your mind or writing it down through journaling. The only way we will truly be able to improve in our practice is if we take the time to think about how we actually lived it on a particular day as well as things we could have done better.

As we live this life of recovery and as a Stoic, we must learn to live in moderation. It is fine to do things to satisfy the body's needs, but we should not spend an immoderate amount of time doing them (we do not want to pick up a new addiction). But the ultimate thing we need to remember is to care for our minds. We need to work out our ability to logically think and reason in situations we face because this will help strengthen our recovery and our growth as a Stoic. We must also take the time to reflect on our journey to see not only the progress we are making but also how we can continue to improve.

"Developing inner values is much like physical exercise. The more we train our abilities, the stronger they become. The difference is that, unlike the body, when it comes to training the mind, there is no limit to how far we can go." – Dalai Lama

CHAPTER 42

When Someone Thinks Wrong of You
(Temperance)

When any person does ill by you, or speaks ill of you, remember that he acts or speaks from an impression that it is right for him to do so. Now it is not possible that he should follow what appears right to you, but only what appears so to himself. Therefore, if he judges from false appearances, he is the person hurt, since he, too, is the person deceived. For if anyone takes a true proposition to be false, the proposition is not hurt, but only the man is deceived. Setting out, then, from these principles, you will meekly bear with a person who reviles you, for you will say upon every occasion, "It seemed so to him." – Chapter 42, Epictetus' Enchiridion.

———

Have you ever had someone say something about you that was not true? How did it make you feel? Angry? Depressed? Ashamed? The emotions it can provoke depend on how well we know the person and what they say. Remembering that one focus of Stoicism is in dealing with the causes of our negative emotions means that we need to find healthy ways to deal with a situation like this.

The first thing that Epictetus reminds us of in this chapter is that when a person speaks or acts, it is because of an impression that seems right to them. An impression is just someone's opinion; it does not mean it is the truth of the situation. This opinion can be without conscious thought or have little evidence to back it up, but it can be based on the way you look, speak, or behave. The problem with life is that even though we want people to see things how we do, that is impossible. People's thoughts and opinions are guided by how they see things. It is another sign of things that are out of our control.

Early in recovery, depending on our past, we can find that people have false impressions about our sobriety and how dedicated we are to changing as a person. For myself, the first time I entered a rehab program and worked on who I was, I had the support of family and friends who truly believed in what I was doing. However, after multiple relapses... broken promises... different rehabs... the impression they had of me changed. When I went through my last bottom, I found that I didn't have anyone believe in me at first, and everyone questioned whether I was serious about it this time or if it would be just like all the other times. I knew things were different, but I had to accept the impressions that others had of me because of my past actions.

The problem that those of us in recovery have is that false impressions can go far beyond our early days of sobriety. For example, in one study, researchers found people had more negative opinions of individuals suffering from addiction than mental illness and that nearly a third felt that recovery is impossible (Johns Hopkins 2014). Much of the negative attitude was because of the view that the addict is a bad or weak person. Therefore, long into our recovery, we may find that some people still have negative impressions and possibly still speak ill of us, even though we might have years of sobriety.

We know that this is wrong. We know that recovery is possible. We know it is not because we are bad or weak. People who have suffered from addiction can change for the better. These things we know are true propositions, while those in the paragraph above are false impressions.

Rather than get angry or bothered by the people who hold those false impressions, Epictetus suggests we should feel bad for them. That person's beliefs do not change what we know to be true and possible. In fact, it sucks to be them since they have been deceived by what they believe. And we do not even know why they have those beliefs. For all we know, they could have seen loved ones suffer and die from addiction for them to think it true. By believing in their false impressions, they must miss out on all the strong and wonderful people we meet in recovery. All the good stories. All the changed lives. It is their loss. So rather than getting angry if you come across a person like this, think, "Well, that's how they see it," as you know how it truly is.

I gave you this as a simple example to understand the meaning of this chapter. Now the goal is to apply this similar tactic whenever you come across any situation in which someone says something about you that you know to be false. Remember that the ultimate punishment for them thinking badly of you is that they have to miss out on the wonderful person that you are. Practicing this will set you free, as no words uttered toward you will ever be able to touch your inner peace.

"Don't waste your energy trying to educate or change opinions; go over, under, through, and opinions will change organically when you're the boss. Or they won't. Who cares? Do your thing, and don't care if they like it." – Tina Fey

Grab Onto the Right Handle
(Justice)

Everything has two handles: one by which it may be borne, another by which it cannot. If your brother acts unjustly, do not lay hold on the affair by the handle of his injustice, for by that it cannot be borne, but rather by the opposite—that he is your brother, that he was brought up with you; and thus you will lay hold on it as it is to be borne. – Chapter 43, Epictetus' Enchiridion.

For any situation that occurs in life, there are multiple perspectives that we can take. And the perspective we eventually decide upon will affect how we respond to the situation physically and how we feel emotionally in the end. If someone close to us (family or friend) does something that we view as wrong or unjust, we have two paths to take in how we will deal with it.

1. Focus on the act itself.
2. Focus on the person.

If we journey down the first path, we can think about the wrongful act that the person did and how it affects us. This path will obviously lead to negative thoughts and feelings about that person. It could even lead to thoughts of retaliating or getting back at them. And the most dangerous part, especially if we let it boil into resentments, is that we could find our own sobriety at risk.

If we choose the second path in which we focus on the person, we can think about who they are and what they mean to us. We remind ourselves how much we care for that person and everything we have been through together. The ultimate thing to remember is that nobody is perfect, and everyone will mess up occasionally.

Besides, have you always been perfect?

I know that in my addictions, I had acted wrong or unjust to almost everyone in my life. It could have been specific actions I did towards them or merely being absent when I should have been there. So how can I grasp onto the handle of the unjust act while simultaneously asking all the people in my life to grasp onto the handle of who I am to them in my recovery?

Therefore, you have two choices to decide when someone you know does something wrong. You can focus on who they are to you or what they did. One path will lead to negative emotions and make it difficult to handle what occurred. The other will allow you to maintain your inner peace and rational mind while making it easier to bear the action.

We do not have to only think of the special relationships we share with friends and family in this Stoic practice, but we can also begin to think of the relationship we have with humanity. We can focus on the fact that we exist on this planet for each other and are all here to help each other through the struggles of life. Basically, we have the option to never choose that handle of the act itself with anyone, but instead decide to always grasp the handle of who the person is.

The true essence of Stoic justice.

Recall that people's impressions are true only to them and that they might have been deceived into thinking something wrong. Remember that people do not choose to do wrong, but at that moment, they feel it is the right action to commit to. And always remember that even though you may live the life of a Stoic, it is one that you choose and may not be one that they have decided for themselves.

In the end, when faced with the unjust actions of anyone in life, choose to grasp onto the handle of their humanity rather than the act itself. Always remember, they are merely a human trying to weave through the struggles of life in a way that they feel is right and proper. Nobody is perfect and perfection is a lifelong pursuit we can always move closer towards but never achieve. If you can begin to practice this daily, you will discover that you can bear the actions of others in a level-headed manner while maintaining your inner tranquility.

"To err is human, to forgive is divine." – Alexander Pope, An Essay on Criticism.

Don't Judge a Book by Its Cover
(Wisdom)

These reasonings have no logical connection: "I am richer than you, therefore I am your superior." "I am more eloquent than you, therefore I am your superior." The true logical connection is rather this: "I am richer than you, therefore my possessions must exceed yours." "I am more eloquent than you, therefore my style must surpass yours." But you, after all, consist neither in property nor in style. – Chapter 44, Epictetus' Enchiridion.

It is so easy to fall into the trap of using outward appearances to make assumptions about a person. For example, if someone is wealthier than you, does this make them a better person than you? Someone speaks and expresses themselves way better than you can ever imagine. Does this mean that they are better than you are?

The problem is that this is something that our minds can naturally do to us.

In our perception of people, and their perceptions of us, the hidden, subliminal mind takes limited data, and creates a picture that seems clear and real, but is actually built largely on unconscious inferences that are made by employing factors such as a person's body language, voice, clothing, appearance, and social category. – Leonard Mlodinow, How We Are Judged By Our Appearance.

Our minds dislike dealing with the unknown, which can be one of the main reasons we are so fixated on the future. We want to know what will happen because there seems to be safety and security in knowing how things will turn out.

Our minds also dislike dealing with the unknown with other people we come across. So, when we meet someone, our unconscious mind goes to work. It tries to gather whatever data it can about that person: how they look, speak, behave, and even their social status. Then our unconscious minds take this limited data along with some educated guesses to develop our conscious perception of that person (Mlodinow 2021). However, this perception of the person we have developed in our mind is based on very little knowledge that we actually have of them.

It could be completely incorrect.

Besides, as Epictetus has stated multiple times: we are not the money we have, the things we own, the clothes we wear, the way we speak, or even the social category we are in life. Just because someone is wealthier and has more valuables does not mean they are superior to you. Some wealthy people in the world are horrible people with poor character. In fact, some people even gain their wealth through unvirtuous acts of fraud and theft. And just because someone knows how to speak well does not mean they are superior. They can fill the words they say with deceptions and manipulations. And there are even people that can speak quite well but have no clue what they are even talking about.

This is important to us in recovery because people who suffer from addiction have been found to have lower self-esteem than non-addicts, and increased self-esteem is a predictor of avoidance of drugs and narcotics (Alavi 2011). For those of us who suffer from low self-esteem, drugs or alcohol became a way to escape the constant negativity of our thoughts or drown away our sorrows.

I know this was true for me.

Through my alcoholism and addictions, I watched the confident person I was in my younger years rapidly wash away to where I thought I was one of the worst human beings to exist on the planet. The lowest of the low. As a result, I had zero self-esteem when I entered rehab after my last bottom.

I was a destroyed human being.

If increased self-esteem is a predictor of avoidance of our drugs of choice, we need to see the world as it truly is. We need to fight our unconscious brain from filling in the gaps and making guesses about other people to determine whether they are superior to us. Instead, we must make the proper conclusions. This is a further expansion of Stoic practices on the judgments that we make in life. We need to separate the outward characteristics of a person from the value judgments we make about what they say about their character.

Someone has more money than you...they are not superior; they just have more money. Someone dresses better than you...they are not superior; they just dress better. Someone speaks better than you...they are not superior; they just speak better.

These are merely external things.

They say nothing of the true person.

The value of a person is in the greatness of their character. And your character is not measured in money, possessions, or how well you speak. If you strive to live a life of virtue, to be the best person you can be every day, then nobody can be your superior. Therefore, we must stop judging our value in relation to others and instead see the value we bring to the world through our existence. Stoicism's power in guiding you to live a better life is that it genuinely makes you priceless in the end.

"Your appearance shouldn't define who you are, and that's what I like — the contrast between people looking like the opposite of what they truly are deep inside." - Matthias Schoenaerts

CHAPTER 45

Stop Assuming the Why
(Wisdom)

Does anyone bathe hastily? Do not say that he does it ill, but hastily. Does anyone drink much wine? Do not say that he does ill, but that he drinks a great deal. For unless you perfectly understand his motives, how should you know if he acts ill? Thus you will not risk yielding to any appearances but such as you fully comprehend. – Chapter 45, Epictetus' Enchiridion.

I n further expanding what he discussed in the previous chapter, Epictetus now focuses on the concepts of judgments we make about a person, but this time on the actions we see them committing. For example, if you witness a person bathing too quickly (a possible sight at an Ancient Roman public bathhouse) or someone who is drinking too much, your mind might jump to the conclusion that something might be wrong with them mentally. I know that as an alcoholic, I will see people drinking in the manner in which I did in my past and assume they must be alcoholics like me without knowing the complete picture of why they may drink like that right now. I am projecting my past and who I am onto someone I don't know well.

Our brains can take two routes when we see someone acting in a certain way. We can see it as being because of their situation at the time (situational attributes), or we can see it as a reflection of a person's character (personality attributes) (Dorrance-Hall 2018). For example, if you say hello to a coworker and they say nothing back to you. Your brain might assume they did not hear, or maybe they are having an unpleasant morning (situational). You could also take another route and think they are just rude (personality). Our brains tend to use situational attributes with people we know (since we know their nature) and personality attributes with those we do not know. But similarly to the last chapter, our brains have too much to think about and dislike dealing with the unknown, so it will decide how to judge an action unconsciously so we can move on to other things. This is one reason Stoicism focuses so much on training and building the strength of your rational mind because our brains do things for us without us even asking them to do it.

For those of us who have suffered from addiction, judging why someone is acting in a certain way can manifest itself in our lives due to:

1. Paranoia
2. Guilt
3. Low Self-Esteem

Paranoia can be this feeling that the world is out to get you, causing feelings of persecution, reluctance to trust others, and seeing intent behind events that most people would recognize as coincidental (UK Rehab n.d.). A person dealing with paranoia is literally trying to read into the actions and intent of others in a manner in which those people are out to get them. Now, paranoia can be directly caused by the drugs that are being consumed and could subside with sobriety. However, it could also be a sign of a mental condition that needs to be treated medically as well.

Guilt can prompt individuals to over-interpret signs of disapproval from others (Winch 2014), closely scrutinizing their actions to find validation for their feelings of guilt. Among those struggling with addiction, guilt may arise from the addiction itself or the actions committed to sustain it. Consequently, individuals suffering from addiction might become hyper-aware of others' behavior, seeking signs of disapproval that reinforce their internalized guilt. This heightened sensitivity to perceived disapproval can further exacerbate feelings of shame and inadequacy, creating a cycle of negative self-perception. Understanding this dynamic is crucial in addressing the emotional complexities that accompany addiction. By recognizing the interplay between guilt, external validation, and self-worth, individuals can take steps toward healing and developing a healthier perspective on themselves and their relationships with others.

People who suffer from low self-esteem seek validation from others to either make themselves feel better about who they are or support those thoughts of low self-esteem. They will try to interpret other people's actions to feed whatever aspect their low self-esteem is craving.

Whether it was paranoia, guilt, or low self-esteem during our addictions that caused us to judge closely the actions of others, we need to make sure that we do our best to end this practice in our recovery.

If our unconscious mind is forcing us to make assumptions about why people do certain things, then there must be something our conscious mind can do to counteract it. This is what Epictetus is discussing for us to do in this chapter. Staying true to the Stoic concept of not making judgments about things, we need to see what people do simply as being what they are doing and nothing else. Using your rational mind, just tell yourself the action you see occurring and do not carry it any deeper. Someone bathes fast...just say they bathe fast. If you see someone overly drunk...just say they drank too much. The coworker does not say hello to you...just say they did not say hello to you.

Embracing this approach may not come easily at first, as you'll be challenging a long-standing aspect of your mind, one that you've relied upon throughout most of your life. Your mind might naturally lean towards making assumptions about people, especially strangers, based on their actions. However, with dedicated practice, you can strengthen your rational mind and develop the ability to see actions at their face value—without rushing to judgments or assumptions. This shift in perspective brings clarity and reduces unnecessary mental turmoil, leaving you with a deeper sense of tranquility in your daily interactions.

"Your assumptions are your windows on the world. Scrub them off every once in a while, or the light won't come in." – Isaac Asimov

CHAPTER 46

Actions Speak Louder Than Words
(Courage, Wisdom)

Never proclaim yourself a philosopher; nor make much talk among the ignorant about your principles, but show them by actions. Thus, at an entertainment, do not discourse how people ought to eat; but eat as you ought. For remember that thus Socrates also universally avoided all ostentation. And when persons came to him, and desired to be introduced by him to philosophers, he took them and introduced them; so well did he bear being overlooked. – Chapter 46, Epictetus' Enchiridion.

D o not go around telling everyone that you are a philosopher. Earlier in the book, Epictetus had warned that if we do something like that, it could invite us to be mocked by others.

At this point, it should be quite apparent that the Stoic way of life differs from how most people live. It discusses changing the things you value in life, seeing the world and other people from a new perspective, battling the natural unconscious tendencies of your mind, and learning to let go of things you may have held closely onto before. But if you ask me, I feel this is the reason Stoicism is quite helpful for those of us in recovery. For many of us, how the world lives and the status quo were insufficient, which could have been one of the possible reasons for our addictions.

If someone is ignorant of the Stoic life that you choose to live, words may not be quite helpful to them initially. They may be totally fine with their view of living life and may not even be open to philosophical ideas. Epictetus warns that you do not want to be that person who is constantly telling people how you do or view things differently than them. It can appear preachy or pretentious, which could turn people against the way you live rather than attract them to it.

The best way to tell people about this Stoic life you choose, or any philosophy you take up, is to show it to them in action. People do not need to hear you talk about how to live life; they need to see it. Nobody knows this better than those of us who have gone through addiction and have chosen to live in recovery. The people in our lives do not want to hear us talk about how we plan to stop and change for the better; they want to see it.

Epictetus then follows this up by referring to Socrates once again because he was known to be a person who did not just speak philosophy; he was a person that fully lived it till his death. Desiring not to attract attention to himself, if someone wanted to meet a philosopher, Socrates would bring them to one rather than declaring out loud he was one. How he lived spoke the loudest of the philosophy that guided his journey through life. It should have been something a person had seen when they approached him to learn.

So if ever there should be among the ignorant any discussion of principles, be for the most part silent. For there is great danger in hastily throwing out what is undigested. And if anyone tells you that you know nothing, and you are not nettled at it, then you may be sure that you have really entered on your work. For sheep do not hastily throw up the grass to show the shepherds how much they have eaten, but, inwardly digesting their food, they produce it outwardly in wool and milk. Thus, therefore, do you not make an exhibition before the ignorant of your principles, but of the actions to which their digestion gives rise. – Chapter 46, Epictetus' Enchiridion.

For this part, I will use my personal experience to illustrate what is being discussed. Long before I had read this chapter, I learned the harsh reality of what was being taught here and why it is important for us to remember the principles in our practice of the philosophy in our interactions with others.

When I first learned about Stoicism, I was excited to tell others. I wanted them to know this new way of looking at the world and how I would live life. I thought it could really help people in life and they should hear about it. And do not get me wrong, I still believe it could help many people, whether or not they are in recovery. I would not be writing this book if I did not think this way.

However, I was doing what Epictetus was warning about here, throwing out undigested ideas and principles. I had just begun reading about Stoicism and had not studied it to the depth I have now.

As a result, I did not realize a deeper understanding of what I was reading. Since I had not fully put the principles into practice, I did not know the extent of what it was trying to say. It is a philosophy of action and not words. Until you truly put it into action, you cannot understand the full extent of its power and the positive effects it can have on your life.

I remember going to different recovery meetings, and when it came to sharing, I wanted to interject what I had been learning. A considerable part of Stoicism interconnects with the Big Book, so I was trying to add to the topics being discussed with the discoveries I had been making. However, not understanding the philosophy to the fullest extent made some of these shares go not too well and actually did a disservice to Stoicism. I was speaking from theory and not from the actual practice of it.

The other problem with spewing it out before we digest it is that you risk looking like you are full of shit. I remember in those early days talking to my girlfriend about what I was reading and this new way of life I would live. But then she found me saying things and acting in ways contradicting Stoic philosophy; she called me out. I was still making judgments about people, getting angry over things I did not have control over, and focusing too much on the future rather than living in the present. As I have said throughout this book, the change to living this life will not be sudden but gradual through practice. And she rightfully called me out on not living the principles by which I said I would live my life.

Epictetus uses this example of sheep to explain the deeper meaning of this chapter. When a sheep is nourished by grass, it does not just spew out what it has consumed undigested to show what it has fed upon. Instead, the sheep digests the nourishment and shows its value outwardly through the wool and milk it produces.

Philosophy nourishes the mind but only shows its importance through the life we live and the actions we choose. Who we become through it is the only way to show the world that it nourishes us appropriately.

My philosophical discussions now are one-on-one with people, allowing for deeper, meaningful conversations. It could be with people who have known me long enough to witness the changes it has made to my life (they see the wool from my digestion) or others who I have known less but note that I respond differently to the world. Sometimes I share out at meetings when someone says something that I think could benefit them. However, now I speak from experience of putting what I say into action rather than just theories I have read. And even my girlfriend, who rightfully pointed out my hypocritical behavior, sees the difference in me. She sees how I react to struggling situations with a calmness that I never had before. So, I never have to say anything about the Stoic life I live or the person I am; instead, the things I do say it for me.

"Words may show a man's wit but actions his meaning."
– Benjamin Franklin

CHAPTER 47

Only You Need to Know
(Courage, Justice)

When you have learned to nourish your body frugally, do not pique yourself upon it; nor, if you drink water, be saying upon every occasion, "I drink water." But first consider how much more frugal are the poor than we, and how much more patient of hardship. If at any time you would inure yourself by exercise to labor and privation, for your own sake and not for the public, do not attempt great feats; but when you are violently thirsty, just rinse your mouth with water, and tell nobody.
– Chapter 47, Epictetus' Enchiridion.

Epictetus continues to build on the concepts discussed in the previous chapter, emphasizing the importance of letting our actions speak for the philosophy we choose to live. He advises against the need to declare our beliefs loudly to the world, as the true purpose of living a meaningful philosophy lies in personal growth and self-improvement—not seeking validation from others or showing off.

The urge to show off can often stem from feelings of insecurity or the desire for acceptance from others, as supported by research

(Parvez 2021). When we reflect on this, it becomes evident that there is no genuine reason to showcase our actions and possessions to others unless seeking a reaction or approval from them. Feelings of insecurity and the need for acceptance are two things that run in contradiction to Stoic philosophy. The focus on character development, living a virtuous life, committing to actions that you know to be right, and realizing your actual value should help fight back feelings of insecurity that we may have once felt through our addictions and early recovery. As for the need for acceptance from others, Stoicism teaches that we have no control over the reputation that others give us and that our feelings toward opinions of us should be something that we are indifferent to. Therefore, to summarize, there is really no reason to show off what we are doing.

Epictetus, as always, provides several examples to illustrate his point. If you choose to embrace a simple and minimalist lifestyle, being frugal with the foods you consume, there is no need to show off these choices to others. In Roman society, where wine consumption was prevalent, someone opting to drink only water might stand out, but that does not necessitate announcing it to everyone. Epictetus humorously points out that such actions are not as extraordinary as some may believe. People living in poverty often have even less and endure greater hardships without feeling the need to seek attention or recognition.

Once again, he brings up the idea of working out, another example of how things never really change. The benefits of working out are so widely known that there is no reason for me to list them here. Exercising is for you and your own health. However, with the rise of social media, there has been an increase in people making social media posts about their workout regimen and images of them every time they go to the gym. Recent research has found that the more frequently someone posts about their workouts on social media, the more likely they exhibit narcissistic behavior with the need for attention and validation (Hoffman, Hunter, and Petter 2021). And even for people who do not do it out of narcissism but as a way to document their fitness journey, their posts have been found to hurt the self-esteem of others who see the posts and then become concerned about their weight and lack of working out (Pesce 2018). Basically, this trend of broadcasting to the world your workout regiment directly contradicts Stoic courage and justice. If it is for narcissistic reasons for attention and validation, it works against the virtue of courage, and if your posts are making others feel bad, it goes against justice. Working out is something for your own good; others do not need to know about it.

In the last part of the chapter, Epictetus points out that despite what we do to live a better life, there is always room for improvement. He discusses this with the example that he gives of not only just drinking water but getting to the level where, in violent thirst, you can survive just by rinsing out your mouth. Stoicism is a lifelong pursuit. We may never become the perfect Stoic sage. After all, we are human, and everyone has their slip-ups. As you change and do things in a new way, do not stop your growth, but continue to look for ways to improve your life.

Ultimately, this chapter is just a last reminder that the things we do in life are for ourselves. We no longer have to seek outside validation from other people; satisfaction with ourselves should be all we need in our pursuits.

"What the superior man seeks is in himself; what the small man seeks is in others." Confucius, The Analects, 15.

CHAPTER 48

How You Can Tell You Are Living It
(Courage, Justice, Temperance, Wisdom)

The condition and characteristic of a vulgar person is that he never looks for either help or harm from himself, but only from externals. The condition and characteristic of a philosopher is that he looks to himself for all help or harm. – Chapter 48, Epictetus' Enchiridion.

———————

Throughout this book, I have discussed many core concepts underlying the Stoic philosophy. I described the overarching goal of a virtuous life. I have gone over the principles that can guide one toward it. I even went over ways that you can actively use it.

So how can you gauge your progress in living as a Stoic?

In this chapter, Epictetus presents some personal checks we can do to see if we are practicing it in our daily lives. Remembering that this is all about progress over perfection, read through this chapter and keep it marked so that you can reread it to give yourself that personal check on how you are doing on your journey.

A vulgar person refers to someone not educated in this philosophy, equating to the world at large. Most people will see that it usually comes from someone else or an outside situation when they are harmed or hurt. And most people seek help from others to get through life's difficulties. This perspective focuses on the idea that harm or help has to come from things outside of us which would be things that are out of our control.

A Stoic lives understanding to look inside themselves for all help and harm. For the idea of help, think of the Stoic Challenge. The problematic situations we are given in life exist to test our abilities and become opportunities to grow. The obstacle is the way, and inside us is the strength to overcome it. When it comes to people harming you, it is your choice whether you have been hurt or not and if you will give them the power to.

"You have the right to make them hurt you, and they don't like to do that." – James Bond Stockdale, Courage Under Fire.

Returning to the example of James Stockdale, the fighter pilot who used Epictetus to survive his imprisonment during the Vietnam War, one powerful realization that occurred to him was that the torturing punishments he had to endure could not harm him. The guards could not have power over him if he chose not to let them. The punishments inflicted on him were coming from another person, but how he would respond to them internally would be entirely up to him.

If you realize that nobody can hurt you unless you allow them to. If you realize that the power to overcome challenges in your path is contained inside of you. Then you are on your way to living a Stoic life.

The marks of a proficient are that he censures no one, praises no one, blames no one, accuses no one; says nothing concerning himself as being anybody or knowing anything. When he is in any instance hindered or restrained, he accuses himself; and if he is praised, he smiles to himself at the person who praises him; and if he is censured, he makes no defense. But he goes about with the caution of a convalescent, careful of interference with anything that is doing well but not yet quite secure. – Chapter 48, Epictetus' Enchiridion.

For the second part of this chapter, Epictetus gives a short checklist of how you interact with other people. We act with other people in so many ways daily, from family and friend interactions, dealing with coworkers or customers, driving on the roads with other people, shopping or going out to eat, and now even on social media. These interactions can dramatically affect our emotional state in the present moment, and throughout this book, numerous ways in which we should handle them have been discussed.

Remember that we do not know the whys behind people's actions or words. We do not know what is happening in someone's life in the present moment that is influencing their current behavior. We also need to remember that sometimes people do things that would seem evil but are just misguided in their thinking. When we look down on others for what they do or say, we need to consider why we do that. The disapproval we are thinking or feeling is a flaw within ourselves, not the other person. Therefore, he says we should not censure other people.

We should also not praise others because we do not know why they do such things. Sometimes people can do what seems to be selfless acts for selfish reasons. You can find numerous examples of wealthy people being involved in philanthropy, but when you look closely at why they are doing it, there is actually a monetary benefit for themselves in the process. Besides, we must consider doing the right thing in life as the expectation, not the exception. It is kind of a sad commentary for the world we live in to have to praise someone for doing something right when that is what they should have been doing anyways.

Similarly, we should not expect praise from others since we do the right things because they are the right thing to do. Often, people will do something good to receive praise for the action. As discussed in the last chapter, people who do things for others to see usually suffer from insecurity or the need for outside validation, which is why we should not expect praise for doing something right. Besides, if we fall into the trap of seeking praise for the good things that we do, what will happen if that praise does not come? Would we still want to do the right thing even though we are not getting out of it what we initially desired?

Finally, and sticking with the same theme in the first part of this chapter, we should not be blaming or accusing anyone of any harm that may have been committed because they do not have the ability to harm us. The only person to blame when we are hurt is ourselves for allowing it to occur.

Reminding us of recent chapters, he discusses how we should not brag about what we do or know. The philosopher's life you live is shown through the actions you do, not the words you say. If someone praises us, we internally smile at what they said and do not go around bragging about it, remembering that our reputation is out of our control and should be something we learn to be indifferent to. If someone criticizes us, we do not defend what we are doing. We are living a life that differs from most others that we are surrounded by and that what we know is the right thing to do may not make sense to them. Finally, if we find ourselves dealing with something that blocks our path to where we want to travel in life, it is not anyone else's fault but ultimately up to us to figure out how we will overcome it and keep progressing.

He finishes this with an analogy that compares how we need to move through life in the same manner as an older person. Be careful in the path you walk, knowing that even though things might go well at the moment, a Stoic challenge can pop up at any time that will test your strength and inner balance. If you deal with other people in the manner described above, you are progressing in living a Stoic life.

He restrains desire; he transfers his aversion to those things only which thwart the proper use of our own will; he employs his energies moderately in all directions; if he appears stupid or ignorant, he does not care; and, in a word, he keeps watch over himself as over an enemy and one in ambush. – Chapter 48, Epictetus' Enchiridion.

The last part of this chapter focuses on the inner self that we are living and striving for. To ensure that we have internalized what we should seek and value in our daily lives.

We know what it means to restrain desire and the importance of it. In recovery, we choose a life dedicated to restraining ourselves from our drug of choice, and we must do that because once we give into it, our addictions take control of our lives. We must restrain our desire because it will become our master. However, we must do this with things other than our drug of choice. It is fine to have goals, but to desire them is to bring them to a different level in which we will not feel satisfied until we have them. The future is out of our control, so desiring things to come to fruition puts us on shaky ground emotionally because of the possibility that they may never happen. We also have to give up our desire for material possessions, knowing that they will not lead to lifetime happiness (hedonic adaptation) and that they can be lost as quickly as they are gained. We also have to check our desires with other people; they control their own lives, so any expectations from them are unknown to us. Ultimately, restraining desire is a practice of controlling our negative emotions, knowing that we give up our control to things we desire, and they then get to rule how we feel inside.

Challenges will arise in life; it's ridiculous not to expect them. When faced with potential adversity, we should prepare ourselves for how we will respond if they occur. Wasting energy on desperately wanting them not to happen is futile, as we have no control over their inevitability. Instead, we should shift our focus inward, concentrating on our inner selves when dealing with undesirable situations. In the journey of recovery, many of us confront the character flaws and weaknesses that lie within us—the very vulnerabilities we may have been evading through addiction. Embracing these flaws is essential, redirecting our aversion towards them. By doing so, we take control over aspects of ourselves that are within our sphere of influence—the realm of our will. This empowers us to grow, evolve, and actively improve ourselves on the path to healing and transformation.

Employing our energies moderately in all directions discusses how we must live a balanced life. It gets at the core concept behind a "work-life balance" in which we make sure to live our lives rather than put it all into work. It also explains the nature of co-dependency and having our relationships take over so much of our lives. Finally, it goes back to that concept that Seneca discussed in which we have long enough lives, but that we waste so much time and energy on all these things that do not truly matter.

Finishing the chapter, Epictetus points out that our only enemy in life is ourselves. Unfortunately, we are our own worst enemy. Something those of us in recovery know all too well. If we let our guard down to our addictions, we risk relapse. Go to enough meetings, and you will eventually hear the stories of people who lost years of sobriety by becoming complacent in their recovery.

Nobody can harm us unless we let them do that. Nobody can take away our inner peace unless we allow them to. The only way they can attack us is if we allow it. Therefore, we realize the enemy is within us, and we must be vigilant in watching for its attack. It is within our power to ensure the enemy does not get the best of us.

If you practice all the principles discussed in this chapter, you are well on your way to living a Stoic life. Of course, some are much more difficult than others, but with time you will hone your skills and get better at them if you are dedicated to doing so—progress not perfection, in this journey that you will travel for the rest of your life.

"The secret of making progress is to get started." – Mark Twain

CHAPTER 49

Knowing Is Not Enough
(Courage, Wisdom)

When anyone shows himself vain on being able to understand and interpret the works of Chrysippus, say to yourself: "Unless Chrysippus had written obscurely, this person would have had nothing to be vain of. But what do I desire? To understand nature, and follow her. I ask, then, who interprets her; and hearing that Chrysippus does, I have recourse to him. I do not understand his writings. I seek, therefore, one to interpret them." So far there is nothing to value myself upon. And when I find an interpreter, what remains is to make use of his instructions. This alone is the valuable thing. But if I admire merely the interpretation, what do I become more than a grammarian, instead of a philosopher, except, indeed, that instead of Homer I interpret Chrysippus? When anyone, therefore, desires me to read Chrysippus to him, I rather blush when I cannot exhibit actions that are harmonious and consonant with his discourse. – Chapter 49, Epictetus' Enchiridion.

P ractice what you preach.

When a common saying exists for something that someone does, it is most likely because many people are guilty of doing such a thing. Have you ever met someone who will loudly say they know the right way to do something, but when you look at their actions, they do not? They might talk about the things they have read or learned that make them an expert on what they are saying, but nothing of what they do shows they actually use that knowledge or advice in their own lives.

Chrysippus was one of the early leaders of Stoic philosophy in Ancient Greece. His written works expanded on the thought and practice of Stoicism and would have been known to Ancient Roman philosophers (like Epictetus).

Epictetus jokingly points out that if someone boasts or brags about knowing all the works of Chrysippus, they obviously do not understand what he is saying because Stoics do not believe in bragging or boasting. So, in essence, the person will not be practicing what they preach merely because they are boasting and bragging.

"According to this view, we all possess certain deep-seated, intuitive, natural, and common sense assumptions but fail to apply them consistently or think their logical implications through." – Donald Robertson, The Philosophy of Cognitive-Behavioral Therapy, pg. 21.

Stoic philosophy believes that there are certain traits (rational thinking being the main one) that all humans have and that we are just not applying them correctly. It is trying to get to the heart of human nature. It then tries to use this understanding and turn it into action to live the good life no matter what situation we find ourselves in. Therefore, someone seeking this philosophy wants to understand who they are better, what they value, and how to navigate the world they live in.

But without action, it is useless.

It is perfectly fine to read Chrysippus, Epictetus, Seneca, or any other Stoic writers. However, as you engage with their works, take a moment to ask yourself if their perspectives on the world and human nature resonate with you. The same applies to recovery programs like 12-step programs, Refuge Recovery, SMART Recovery, and others. Evaluate whether their insights about your addictions make sense to you. This concept aligns with Epictetus' notion of an "interpreter of human nature." Once you find an interpreter whose teachings align with your understanding, it is time to put their instructions into action. It is not enough to passively absorb knowledge; true transformation occurs when you actively apply their insights to your life.

A person can have every Stoic writer memorized, but unless they are living it, they are not a philosopher of it. Likewise, a person can have the entire Big Book memorized, but without living it, that serves no purpose for them. The same goes for any recovery program that we choose to follow. As Epictetus points out, without putting the words into action, reading these books does not differ from reading any work of fiction. All that you are is a person who is good at reading and discussing what you have read, whether it is fiction or non-fiction.

The final part of this chapter returns to something Epictetus has discussed on multiple occasions. We should see the written works of Stoicism through the actions that you are doing (remember the sheep and the wool). Your life and how you live it teaches the philosophy to others more than any book could do. So do not be that person who goes around telling everyone the knowledge you have; be that person who *shows* everyone what you know.

"Rather than wait to be discovered, discover yourself. Whatever it is that you intend to do later, start doing it now, get good at it, and show people what you've done. Actions speak louder than words."
– Steve-O

CHAPTER 50

Don't Break Your Laws
(Courage)

Whatever rules you have adopted, abide by them as laws, and as if you would be impious to transgress them; and do not regard what anyone says of you, for this, after all, is no concern of yours. – Chapter 50, Epictetus' Enchiridion.

M ost people (nearly 80%) quit their New Year's resolutions by February. Just one month to abandon the goal they laid out for themselves to improve their lives positively. More interesting is that one in seven people never even thought they would see it through. Some quit because of societal pressure (40%), and the average American would spend $15,748.19 to have someone keep them accountable (Gervis 2020). Therefore, people are setting goals they never expect to achieve, cave into peer pressure, and would pay someone to make them accountable for keeping their goals instead of finding accountability inside themselves. It is kind of sad when you think about the fact that a person is self-identifying a way in which they need to improve in life and then quit it within a month.

Epictetus suggests in this chapter that when we tell ourselves about specific goals we may have in life or principles (like Stoicism) by which we say we are going to live, we need to think of them as if they were law. He even raises it to a higher level and says we should act like it is a sacrilegious act against God.

Whether or not you believe in God, the point should be obvious. We know that there are laws we need to follow, and we do our best to obey them. I know that sometimes in our addiction, we may not care to follow them (I know I am guilty of this), but in our recovery, we should live a life in which we respect and try not to break them. And if you are a religious person, there are certain things that your faith may tell you that you should not be doing, and you probably respect them and try to obey them. In fact, most of us feel a sense of guilt when we break the laws of our government or that of our religion.

If laws and faith can shape how we act and behave, why should we treat the goals we have for ourselves and the principles we choose to live by differently? If we know it is to better ourselves, then why should we think of them differently than any law that exists for society's betterment? They are basically the same thing; it is just that, in this case, we get to choose the goals and principles that we feel are right for us to live by.

He then returns to the idea that we need to do this with no concern over the opinions that others might have. The fact that around 40% of people quit their resolutions due to pressure from others shows why he keeps returning to this concept. Sadly, we live in a world where someone can choose something to better themselves and where others destroy their ability to achieve it. Therefore, we need to build our strength, not care what others think, and only focus on what we feel about ourselves.

It is in your power to choose the goals you have and the principles you live by. And unless you are lying to yourself, you know it is something you need. So do not give up on them so quickly. Instead, treat them as laws that have consequences for breaking. And do not let anyone pressure you into breaking your own laws.

"I want freedom and I realize that the only way to get it is to quit breaking the law." – Gary Gilmore

CHAPTER 51

The Time Is Now
(Courage)

How long, then, will you delay to demand of yourself the noblest improvements, and in no instance to transgress the judgments of reason? You have received the philosophic principles with which you ought to be conversant; and you have been conversant with them. For what other master, then, do you wait as an excuse for this delay in self-reformation? You are no longer a boy but a grown man. If, therefore, you will be negligent and slothful, and always add procrastination to procrastination, purpose to purpose, and fix day after day in which you will attend to yourself, you will insensibly continue to accomplish nothing and, living and dying, remain of vulgar mind. – Chapter 51, Epictetus' Enchiridion.

D o you have any somedays-you-will in your mind? Someday I will travel more. Someday I would like to change careers. Someday I would like to learn about a certain hobby. Someday I will do this. Someday I will do that.

Sometimes it feels so easy to fill our lives with somedays…

...rather than simply do.

"Can anything be sillier than the point of view of certain people—I mean those who boast of their foresight? They keep themselves very busily engaged in order that they may be able to live better; they spend life in making ready to live! They form their purposes with a view to the distant future; yet postponement is the greatest waste of life; it deprives them of each day as it comes, it snatches from them the present by promising something hereafter."
– Seneca, On the Shortness of Life, Chapter IX.

This quote from Seneca instantly affected me the moment I read it. In fact, his entire work, *On the Shortness of Life,* will change your perspective on how you will live your present moment. It is ridiculous to think of the concept of someday as if we have the ability to know that someday will ever come. The only thing we have in our possession is the present moment, and the next moment will always be a gift. Life can end for any of us in the blink of an eye, and all those somedays will be instantly gone and never fulfilled. We spend our entire lives keeping ourselves busy in order to live better eventually, or as he pointed out, we "spend our life in making ready to live." And the greatest waste of life we can have is a list of somedays-we-will with very few actually dids. Finally, we come to our final days, discovering that we had never truly lived.

"Waste no more time arguing what a good man should be. Be one." – Marcus Aurelius, Meditations, 10:16.

Those of us who have lived with addiction know the importance of wasting no more time. You or someone you may have known might have said they would quit in a day...week...month—just a little bit more time to live in addiction. But nothing can say we will survive that day…week…month. One more day in our addiction may be too much. Staying at my sober living for several years now, I have witnessed multiple occasions where someone who had relapsed said they would be back in a few days after they cleaned up, not to survive that long. I even gave someone a ride to a place where he could stay as he cleaned up before he could return. But unfortunately, I would learn days later that he had overdosed that same night. The guilt of this situation was difficult to overcome as I struggled with what I could have said differently during that car ride or where I could have taken him instead.

The time is now to live a good life. The time is now to live a virtuous life. The time is now to be a good person. Throughout this book, you have learned the Stoic principles and ways to practice them. You have learned the guide to the good life and the tranquility it will bring. But, as Epictetus points out, you aren't getting any younger ("You are no longer a boy, but a grown man"). And you cannot make this one of those somedays, procrastinating on when you will start to live this way—waiting for some time in the future when it will be easier to create the changes in your life to live this new way, finding excuse after excuse why you cannot do it right now. The problem with this mindset is that you risk coming to the end of your life and discovering that you have used so many excuses to push it off to another day that you never got the chance to live a good life.

This instant, then, think yourself worthy of living as a man grown up and a proficient. Let whatever appears to be the best be to you an inviolable law. And if any instance of pain or pleasure, glory or disgrace, be set before you, remember that now is the combat, now the Olympiad comes on, nor can it be put off; and that by one failure and defeat honor may be lost or—won. Thus Socrates became perfect, improving himself by everything, following reason alone. And though you are not yet a Socrates, you ought, however, to live as one seeking to be a Socrates. – Chapter 51, Epictetus' Enchiridion.

———

Continuing with this concept of the time is now, Epictetus discusses you are ready to live the philosopher's life. This could be the first book of Stoicism that you have read, but you should have read enough to begin implementing it in your own life. Authentic learning takes place through living it and improving through experience.

"The philosopher lives in an intermediate state. He is not a sage, but he is not a non-sage, either. He is therefore constantly torn between the non-philosophical life and the philosophical life, between the habitual and everyday, on the one hand, and, on the other, the domain of consciousness and lucidity." – Pierre Hadot, Philosophy as a Way of Life, pg. 103.

We will most likely never hit that perfection of the sage, but it is not like we are not sage-like at all if we choose to live this way. As Epictetus points out, Socrates was not always perfect in what he practiced but became the philosopher he was by improving himself through all his experiences and using his rational mind. And even though we may not be at his level, there is no reason that we cannot aim for it. Therefore, choosing what you have learned throughout this book and what you think will help you live the best possible life should now become laws you refuse to break from this point on. It will be sacrilegious for you not to live the way you decide is best for you.

Life is a battle.

The championship game is here.

Today is the day you decide how you will fight in combat.

Today is the day you decide how well you play the game.

"Change your life today. Don't gamble on the future, act now, without delay." – Simone de Beauvoir

CHAPTER 52

Focus on Doing First and Foremost
(Courage, Justice, Temperance, Wisdom)

The first and most necessary topic in philosophy is the practical application of principles, as, We ought not to lie; the second is that of demonstrations as, Why it is that we ought not to lie; the third, that which gives strength and logical connection to the other two, as, Why this is a demonstration. For what is demonstration? What is a consequence? What a contradiction? What truth? What falsehood? The third point is then necessary on account of the second; and the second on account of the first. But the most necessary, and that whereon we ought to rest, is the first. But we do just the contrary. For we spend all our time on the third point and employ all our diligence about that, and entirely neglect the first. Therefore, at the same time that we lie, we are very ready to show how it is demonstrated that lying is wrong. – Chapter 52, Epictetus' Enchiridion.

Throughout this book, I have discussed the philosophy of Stoicism in several ways. I presented you with ways to practically apply the philosophy, arguments, and evidence for why you should do things in that manner.

Epictetus presents the three fundamental ways we should look at applying philosophy in this second to the last chapter. He says the first is the practical application of the principles of that philosophy or simply what we are to do or not do. The second part is the arguments (demonstrations) for why we should do or not do that. The last component is how the arguments support the practical application. Basically, do the arguments for why we should do or not do something make sense? He discusses how the third is necessary since we have to support why the arguments are good, and the second is essential because we have to justify why we would apply that principle in our daily lives.

He then provides an example. The first part would simply say we should not lie. The second part would be the argument of why we should not lie. And the third part would be how the arguments support we should not lie. I will give another example from Stoicism. The first part is that we should not concern ourselves with the opinions of others. The second part would be that the opinions of others are out of our control. The third part would think of what happens when I let the opinions of others get to me, reminding myself of the things I have control over and do not, and remembering that I should only be concerned with what I have control over.

The reason Epictetus is presenting this information is simply because of how human nature works. People always want to know the reason they should do something. It can be frustrating to be told to do something, and you do not see why you should do it. The moral dilemma of wondering if it is okay to follow a law that you find unjust has been around for a long time. Even Socrates was put to death fighting a law he did not feel was right. Therefore, the second and third parts are important because they answer the underlying reasons why we do things and choose to live by the principles we select to guide us.

However, Epictetus points out that the most crucial part is the first one, the actual application of the principle. It is the doing that matters the most. But we often get into this tendency to focus all our time on arguing on the third point of providing evidence of why or why not we should do something. It is very similar to being a parent and raising a kid. You will tell your kid to do or not do something, and they will ask why. You will give the argument to answer that question. And then they ask why again, pushing you to the third part where you have to say why your first reason was right. And you can get stuck in this pattern of having to keep providing more evidence while, at the end of the day, you just want your child to apply the principle you are telling them to.

We need to not act like children.

Remember, we are grown, and the time is now.

It reminds me of an interaction I had with my brother during my addiction. He gave me the first part, telling me I should get help and stop drinking. His second part was I have a problem with alcohol and might be an alcoholic. And like how they say some of us can act like children in our addictions, I argued with him using the third part. Saying he drinks too, so how could he say anything about me? Asking him how do I know he is not an alcoholic? I spent so much time on part three I didn't even get to part one, which would be simply looking at the fact that I had an issue with alcohol and needed to stop drinking.

This leads to the last part of this chapter and why the saying "do as I say, not as I do" exists. People can get so caught up in focusing on the arguments that we can provide someone with the reasons they should do something (or not do) without doing it themselves. Or, as Epictetus points out, we can give them all the reasons they should not lie while we continue to lie the whole time. As discussed so often throughout this book, Stoicism is a philosophy of action; the why will never be as important as the actual doing.

"Right action is better than knowledge; but in order to do what is right, we must know what is right." – Charlemagne

CHAPTER 53

What Guides Epictetus
(Wisdom)

Upon all occasions, we ought to have these maxims ready at hand: -

"Conduct me, Zeus, and thou, O Destiny,
Wherever your decrees have fixed my lot.
I follow cheerfully; and, did I not,
Wicked and wretched, I must follow still."
Cleanthes – Diogenes Laertius

"Whoe'er yields properly to Fate is deemed
Wise among men, and knows the laws of Heaven."
Euripides – Fragments

And this third:

"O Crito, if it thus pleases the gods, thus let it be."
Plato – Crito

"Anytus and Melitus may kill me indeed; but hurt me they cannot."
Plato – Apology

In every chapter of this book, I presented various quotes that I found useful in my journey as a Stoic and in my recovery. Epictetus had quotes from others in which he had found value which he presents here in this chapter. You have learned enough throughout these pages to see why he particularly enjoyed these few. You no longer need my guidance to be enlightened.

I hope you have gained a greater understanding of Stoicism as you read this book and see how it can help you with your lifelong recovery journey. Whether or not you choose to follow the Stoic path, I urge you to discover what your philosophy of life will be and live it. You do not want to come to the end of your life to discover that you have mislived the one that you have been blessed with. We might have burned through time throughout our addictions, but in sobriety we can now embrace what time we have left and make the most of it. Thank you for spending your present moments reading this book; I hope you found value in it.

Remember, the time is now to live.

The world needs you.

And the good life is in your control.

Literature Cited

Alcoholics Anonymous. *Alcoholics Anonymous*. New York City, N.Y.: Works Publishing / Alcoholics Anonymous World Services, Inc.

Alavi, Hamid Reza. "The Role of Self-esteem in Tendency towards Drugs, Theft and Prostitution." *Addict Health.* 3, 3-4 (2011 Summer-Autumn): 119–124.

American Addiction Centers. "The Link Between Grief and Addiction." Last modified January, 7 2022. https://www.healthdirect.gov.au/grief-loss.

American Society of Plastic Surgeons. "Plastic Surgery Statistics." Accessed on July 15, 2022. https://www.plasticsurgery.org/news/plastic-surgery-statistics

Amodeo, John. "Why Pride is Nothing to Be Proud Of." June 6, 2015. Psychology Today. https://www.psychologytoday.com/us/blog/intimacy-path-toward-spirituality/201506/why-pride-is-nothing-be-proud

Associated Press. "Americans Are the Unhappiest They've Been in 50 Years, Poll Finds." NBC News. June 16, 2020. https://www.nbcnews.com/politics/politics-news/americans-are-unhappiest-they-ve-been-50-years-poll-finds-n1231153.

Aurelius, Marcus. *Meditations*. UK: Penguin Books. 2006.

Baer, Drake. "The 'Maternal Bereavement Effect' Explains Why So Many Parents Die After Their Children." The Cut. December 30, 2016. https://www.thecut.com/2016/12/why-parents-pass-away-if-their-children-die.html.

Blundell, Andrea. "Why We Put the Blame On Others – and the Real Cost We Pay." Harley Therapy. September 10, 2015. https://www.harleytherapy.co.uk/counselling/why-we-put-the-blame-on-others.htm

Bradford Health Services. "The Link Between Drug Addiction and Sexual Addiction." Accessed April 5, 2022. https://bradfordhealth.com/the-link-between-drug-addiction-and-sexual-addiction/

Browne, Rachel. "Young, rich people have higher rates of depression and anxiety, says study." The Sydney Morning Herald. December 8, 2013. https://www.smh.com.au/national/Young-rich-people-have-higher-rates-of-depression-and-anxiety-says-study-20131207-2yy6t.html

Cikanavicius, Darius. "The Trap of External Validation for Self-Esteem." Psych Central. August 2017. https://psychcentral.com/blog/psychology-self/2017/08/validation-self-esteem#1

Choat, Isabel. "Stop Dumping Your Cast-Offs on Us, Ghanaian Clothes Traders Tell EU." The Guardian, 31 May 2023, www.theguardian.com/global-development/2023/may/31/stop-dumping-your-cast-offs-on-us-ghanaian-clothes-traders-tell-eu.

Dorrance-Hall, Elizabeth. "Why We Judge Others." Psychology Today. May 11, 2018. https://www.psychologytoday.com/us/blog/conscious-communication/201805/why-we-judge-others

Epictetus. *The Enchiridion.* Accessed December 17, 2022. https://www.gutenberg.org/files/45109/45109-h/45109-h.htm.

Gaba, Sherry. "All-or-Nothing Thinking in Addiction". Psychology Today. June 25, 2019. https://www.psychologytoday.com/us/blog/addiction-and-recovery/201906/All-or-nothing-thinking-in-addiction

Gervis, Zoya. "The average American abandons their New Year's resolution by this date." New York Post. January 28, 2020. https://nypost.com/2020/01/28/the-average-american-abandons-their-new-years-resolution-by-this-date/

Guzman, Zack. "This Company Will Freeze Your Dead Body for $200,000." NBC News. April 26, 2016. https://www.nbcnews.com/tech/innovation/company-will-freeze-your-dead-body-200-000-n562551

Hadot, Pierre, and Arnold I. Davidson. *Philosophy as a Way of Life.* Oxford: Blackwell. 1995.

HealthDirect Australia. "Grief and Loss." Accessed March 28, 2022. https://www.healthdirect.gov.au/grief-loss.

Hoffmann, Sabrina, John Stanley Hunter and Olivia Petter. "People who post their fitness routines to Facebook have narcissistic traits, study claims." Independent. September 1, 2021.

https://www.independent.co.uk/life-style/fitness-routine-online-facebook-narcissistic-b1912423.html

Irvine, William B. *A Guide to the Good Life*. New York: Oxford University Press. 2009.

Irvine, William B. *The Stoic Challenge*. New York: W.W. Norton and Company. 2019.

John Hopkins. "Study: Public Feels More Negative Toward People With Drug Addiction Than Those With Mental Illness." October 1, 2024. https://publichealth.jhu.edu/2014/Study-public-feels-more-negative-toward-people-with-drug-addiction-than-those-with-mental-illness

Jones, Matthew. "11 Billion Reasons the Self Help Industry Doesn't Want You to Know the Truth about Happiness." Inc.com. October 19, 2017. https://www.inc.com/matthewjones/11-billion-reasons-self-help-industry-doesnt-want-you-to-know-truth-abouthappiness.html.

Kentucky Counseling Center. "5 Minimalist Lifestyle Benefits: There Can Be More with Less" July 20, 2021. https://kentuckycounselingcenter.com/5-minimalist-lifestyle-benefits/

King University. "The Psychology of Social Media." September 19, 2019. https://online.king.edu/news/psychology-of-social-media/

Leifman, Hakan, Charlotta Rehnman, Erika Sjöblom, and Stefan Holgersson. "Anabolic Androgenic Steroids—Use and

Correlates among Gym Users—An Assessment Study Using Questionnaires and Observations at Gyms in the Stockholm Region." *International Journal of Environmental Research and Public Health*. v8, 7 (July 2011): 2656–2674.

Lewis, Tanya. "9 sneaky psychology tricks companies use to get you to buy stuff." Insider. February 10, 2016. https://www.businessinsider.com/9-sneaky-psychology-tricks-companies-use-to-get-you-to-buy-stuff-2016-2

Lutz, Ashley. "Inside the lives of America's anxious wealthy people." Insider. November 8, 2017. https://www.businessinsider.com/habits-richest-people-wealthy-families-anxiety-2017-11

Medindia. "World Death Clock." Accessed May 15, 2022. https://www.medindia.net/patients/calculators/world-death-clock.asp

Milios, Rita. "Control Freak: How to Stop Trying to Change Your World and Change Yourself Instead." American Addiction Centers. Last modified on December 18, 2019. https://recovery.org/pro/articles/control-freak-how-to-stop-trying-to-change-your-world-and-change-yourself-instead/

Mlodinow, Leonard. "How We Are Judged by Our Appearance." Psychology Today. June 11, 2012. https://www.psychologytoday.com/us/blog/subliminal/201206/how-we-are-judged-our-appearance

Northstar Transitions. "Developing and Maintaining a Healthy Daily Schedule in Recovery." August 20, 2020. https://www.northstartransitions.com/post/developing-maintaining-a-healthy-daily-schedule-in-recovery

Northwestern. "Managing the Effects of Social Media on Teen Girls." March 11, 2020. https://counseling.northwestern.edu/blog/effects-social-media-teen-girls/

Parvez, Hanan. "The psychology of people who show off." PsychMechanics. May 18, 2021. https://www.psychmechanics.com/people-who-show-off/

Pesce, Nicole Lyn. "Your daily workout posts are driving your friends crazy." MarketWatch. February 26, 2018. https://www.marketwatch.com/story/your-daily-workout-posts-are-driving-your-friends-crazy-2018-02-26

Pew Research Center. "Religious Landscape Study." Pew Research Center's Religion &Public Life Project. 2021. https://www.pewresearch.org/religion/religious-landscapestudy/.

Reshanov, Alex. "Getting fewer 'likes' on social media can make teens anxious and depressed." University of Rochester. September 24, 2020. https://www.rochester.edu/newscenter/getting-fewer-likes-on-social-media-can-make-teens-anxious-and-depressed-453482/

Robertson, Donald. *Stoicism and the Art of Happiness*. UK: Teach Yourself. 2018

Robertson, Donald. *The Philosophy of Cognitive-Behavioural Therapy (CBT)*. New York: Routledge. 2020.

Rufus, Musonius. *Musonius Rufus: Lectures and Sayings*. Create Space. 2011

Salzgeber, Jonas. *The Little Book of Stoicism: Timeless Wisdom to Gain Resilience, Confidence, and Calmness*. 2019

Seneca and Campbell, Robin. *Letters from a Stoic*. London: Penguin Books. 2004

Seneca. *Of a Happy Life*. https://www.gutenberg.org/files/56075/56075-h/56075-h.htm

Seneca. *On Anger*. The Augustine Press. 2020

Seneca. *On Old Age*. https://commonreader.wustl.edu/c/on-old-age/

Seneca. *On the Shortness of Life*. The Augustine Press. 2019

Sheridan, Kate. "Rich countries are more anxious than poorer countries." Stat. March 15, 2017. https://www.statnews.com/2017/03/15/anxiety-rich-country-poor-country/

Stockdale, James Bond. *Courage Under Fire: Testing Epictetus's Doctrines in a Laboratory of Human Behavior*. Stanford, CA: Hoover Institution on War, Revolution and Peace. 1993.

UK Rehab. "Signs & Symptoms of Addiction – Paranoia." Accessed on July 16, 2022. https://www.uk-rehab.com/addiction/signs-symptoms/paranoia/

Umberson, Debra. "Black Deaths Matter: Race, Relationship Loss, and Effects on Survivors." *Journal of Health and Social Behavior*, 58, no. 4 (December 2017): 405-420. https://journals.sagepub.com/doi/10.1177/0022146517739317.

Watts, Alan. *The Book: On the Taboo Against Knowing Who You Are.* New York: Vintage Books.1966

Winch, Guy. "10 Things You Didn't Know About Guilt." Psychology Today. November 9, 2014. https://www.psychologytoday.com/us/blog/the-squeaky-wheel/201411/10-things-you-didnt-know-about-guilt

Made in the USA
Middletown, DE
10 October 2023

40512482R00176